CONVERSATIONAL SIGN LANGUAGE II

An Intermediate-Advanced Manual

Willard J. Madsen
Associate Professor of Sign Communication

Illustrated by
Ralph R. Miller, Sr.

 Gallaudet College Press
Washington, D.C. 20002

ISBN 0-913580-00-7

TO MY CHILDREN...

Debbie and Lawrence

ABOUT THE AUTHOR

The author of this book, Willard J. Madsen, is Associate Professor of Sign Communication in the School of Communication at Gallaudet College in Washington, D.C., the world's only liberal arts college for the deaf.

A native Kansan and the sixth in a family of ten children, Mr. Madsen was deafened in early childhood by high fever at about the age of two. He attended rural school and the public schools of Peabody, Kansas, through the eighth grade and received his high school education from the Kansas School for the Deaf where he was graduated with top honors in 1947. He was awarded a Bachelor of Arts With Distinction degree from Gallaudet College in 1952 where he had majored in education and where he also achieved top academic honors.

Mr. Madsen earned a Master of Education degree from Louisiana State University in Baton Rouge in 1956, becoming the third deaf person in history at the time to have obtained a degree from that institution and the second to have received a degree in education. He has also done some post-graduate study on the doctoral level at the University of Maryland. Mr. Madsen taught at the Louisiana State School for the Deaf in Baton Rouge from 1952 until 1957 and has since served Gallaudet through the Preparatory Department, the Tutorial Center, the English Department, and Outreach of the Division of Public Services. He also served as Director of Sign Language Programs from its inception in 1971 through 1977. In this capacity, he was responsible for initiating the formal training of interpreters at Gallaudet and for helping to establish a model for the training and certification of teachers of Sign Language. In addition to present duties with the Department of Sign Communication, Mr. Madsen continues to teach journalism and to advise the student newspaper, **The Buff and Blue**.

The author has been associated with Sign Language programs on the Gallaudet campus since the first evening courses were offered by the District of Columbia Association of the Deaf in 1961, and later the National Association of the Deaf (NAD). His original unpublished **Conversational Sign Language** was a product of his first few years of teaching manual communication courses. The work marked the first time that idiomatic signs were ever written up for instructional purposes and was the result of a lack of teaching material for intermediate and advanced courses in sign language. This unique work was first published in 1972 as an expanded text under the title, **Conversational Sign Language II**. It is now in its ninth printing.

Sign Language has not been the author's sole literary interest as he has also written numerous poems since college days, a few of which have also been published. His poem "Idealism" was published in 1951 in the first anthology of college poetry by the National Poetry Association and, more recently, his "You Have to be Deaf to Understand" has appeared in school publications, magazines, and newspapers throughout the country, in Canada, and in other English-speaking countries. It has also been translated into at least seven other languages.

TABLE OF CONTENTS

vi

LIST OF ILLUSTRATIONS

PART I

PART II

PART III

AUTHOR'S PREFACE

Conversational Sign Language II, An Intermediate-Advanced Manual, is the outgrowth of a previously mimeographed text designed for the intermediate student of sign language which was produced under the title **Conversational Sign Language,** in 1967. Like its forerunner, **Conversational Sign Language II** is a text divided into three parts: I — "A Review of Basic Signs and Fingerspelling," II — "English Idioms in Sign Language," and III — "Sign Language Idioms." This is basically where the similarity ends.

Part I in this edition consists of 30 lessons covering a total of approximately 750 English words and their interpretation into signs. These lessons are an expansion of "Helpful Hints and Aids for Better Manual Communication" which the author originally created. Each lesson has its own follow-up exercises to give the student practice material of which there is rarely enough in most books. In addition, a practice test follows every three lessons. These tests are intended to give the student opportunities to reinforce his learning of the signs by means of self-help testing. The student is encouraged to try the practice tests without referring back to the previous three lessons until after he has finished the task.

This section of the book begins with three lessons in fingerspelling designed to assist the student in improving his skills in this area. These three lessons also are followed by a practice test. Illustrations on problems of signing numbers, figures, addresses, telephone numbers, years, fractions, and percentages are retained although these have been revised by artist, Ralph R. Miller, Sr., who also designed the cover and selected illustrations that appear in all three parts of the book. All illustrations in Part I are presented in straight English syntax.

The second section, dealing with the interpretation of English idioms into the language of signs, follows the basic pattern set in Part I. Here, however, are 15 lessons of some 220 English idioms which have been expanded into over 300 usages in sign language. Each lesson contains its own exercises and practice tests follow every three lessons. The five illustrations in Part II appear in precise sign language syntax as far as the English idioms go. One feature of the revised material here is an attempt to rewrite practice material so that it can be covered in a classroom situation in convenient time slots. The three ladies created by the author previously continue to dominate this section and are, for the first time, portrayed in the illustrations. Jacqueline, Josephine, and Geraldine, therefore, do come alive in effect.

The final section of the text deals with the ultimate in genuine conversational sign language in that it presents the colloquialisms that are so prevalent in informal conversational situations among the deaf themselves. Over 300 sign language idioms and colloquialisms are described according to common pattern. This marks the first known attempt to present sign language idioms by pattern as closely as possible. The simpler patterns are presented first and the more complicated ones near the end of the 18 lesson section. By "complicated idioms", we mean those which cannot be presented in any way other than a graphic description of how the expression is formed on the hand or hands. The simpler idioms may be presented in broken English patterns because it is possible to give the student individual English words for which he knows the basic signs and it is possible to give these in the order in which they may be signed, thus creating an idiomatic expression in the language of signs. As in the preceding parts, exercises and practice tests follow the lessons. The five illustrations provided in Part III are strictly in colloquial sign language syntax, but are accompanied by translations into English equivalents. All of the idioms in each lesson are likewise accompanied by equivalent expressions in English so that the student may relate the expressions to language patterns that he knows already. The exercises and practice tests are presented in English and are designed so that the student may translate sentences into sign language idioms or colloquialisms.

Finally an index to Parts I and II and a separate index to Part III are provided since it would be impractical to attempt to incorporate sign language expressions into a regular index of English words. A bibliography rounds out the new edition.

The author wishes to express thanks to those persons who contributed in many ways to the revision and compilation of new material for **Conversational Sign Language II.**

INTRODUCTION

Conversational Sign Language II meets a need which has been expressed by students who study manual communication. Through its evening sign language program, Gallaudet College has enabled hundreds of hearing people in the Washington metropolitan area to learn signs and to be exposed to deafness. The fact that more than 300 persons enrolled in the program during the spring semester of 1972 demonstrates the increasing awareness of the hearing public about deafness and the special needs of deaf people.

Yet it is a common complaint, among learners of formal sign language, that whereas they spend many hours with signs and they express themselves and read others reasonably well in the classroom, they cannot understand the "deaf man on the street" or they cannot understand social conversations outside the formal confines of the classroom. The best solution to this problem would, of course, require total immersion with a deaf family or on the campus of a residential school for deaf students. This book represents a way for the vast majority of students who cannot afford such an investment in time, to study the language as it is actually used by most deaf people. Mr. Madsen's materials have evolved from his long experience as a residential school teacher, actor, college faculty member, sign language instructor, and his present assignment as Coordinator of the Gallaudet College Sign Language Programs. This book meets a long unmet need and will prove to be invaluable to teachers, professional workers, prospective interpreters, and the general public as they progress from formal sign language and fingerspelling to the language as it is communicated in the deaf community.

John S. Schuchman, Ph.D.
Vice President for Academic Affairs
Gallaudet College

NOTE TO THE INSTRUCTOR

Conversational Sign Language II is a manual designed to help both the instructor and the student although it is not entirely a practical self-teaching text. There is greater flexibility for the instructor as Parts I, II, and III may constitute three separate courses in any given program as they are at Gallaudet College.

The 30 lessons in Part I not only reinforce the basic vocabulary usually taught in beginning levels, but actually add to it and the exercises following each lesson enhance the conversational element since each of the signs may be used in some contextual structure. The updating of certain basic signs, the additional vocabulary not available in most basic texts, and the inclusion of some of the newer innovations developed by the S.E.E. (Seeing Essential English) group makes it possible for teacher and student to acquire some insight into happenings in the field. By no means; however, is the inclusion of the latter an endorsement of the basic S.E.E. philosophy. The forms of the verb "to be" and the common prefixes and suffixes are excellent vehicles for communication in manual English and are included for that purpose only. Parent groups and teachers frequently ask for information on such innovations.

In all three parts, the exercises following each lesson provide ready-made material for both the instructor and the student. The exercises can also be used as models for the development of additional practice material, if desired. The practice tests, as stated in the author's preface, may be used more or less as a self-help device. The instructor, too, may use these tests for added receptive practice by presenting the material in a mixed order. This procedure cannot be overemphasized as experience has clearly shown that inadequate receptive practice literally defeats any good course or program.

It is important to recognize, in the absence of adequate standardization of American Sign Language, that there are bound to be differences of opinion on how certain signs should be made. In addition, there are regional differences to tend with in much the same way there are regional dialects in spoken language. It is, therefore, the instructor's responsibility to allow for such differences and, where possible, to explain them the best he or she can. Through several years of teaching experience, the author found that there is a need to point out subtle differences in similar signs in order to help the student over difficult and often confusing situations encountered in the retention of signs. There is of course no substitute for as much experience and contact as possible with deaf adults and deaf people themselves.

The second and third parts should enable a student to acquire a workable knowledge and understanding of the American Sign Language as a language in its own right. **Ameslan** as it is coming to be known today takes into account the sign language structure of the deaf themselves. While there is a need for signed English and manual English and other adaptations plus simultaneous communication, one cannot truly become "well-versed" in American Sign Language or Ameslan without knowing and understanding the colloquialisms peculiar to it. The greatly expanded idiomatic vocabulary in Part III and its presentation in pattern should make such easier to teach and easier to learn. This is the author's primary concern.

NOTE TO THE STUDENT

Congratulations on having come this far! In these pages you will find much new material to guide you along exciting experiences in further advancing your quest to learn the fascinating language of signs as a second language. You are cautioned to give careful attention to the mastering of clear and fluent finger-spelling, both expressively and receptively, as you move from one level to another. Only constant practice in actual communication situations will help you to achieve this, so practice with anyone else who also knows and uses manual communication to help you achieve this goal. You should seek, too, to ask your instructor for help and suggestions on how to get additional receptive practice.

If you take the time to read the "Note to the Instructor", you will see that a number of suggestions have been made for both you and your teacher. Flexibility is the key to successful use of this manual and we encourage acceptance of this as the keynote to your progress and success in acquiring advanced skill in communicating with the deaf in whatever way you choose as long as real communication takes place. Just remember that communication in any language is a two-way street. The language must be learned and used as the "natives" use it. It is the author's fond hope that this book helps you along the way in that vital step.

You may find that the idioms give you some trouble at first, but this is because they are "foreign". Eventually, you should get the "hang of it" and enjoy conversing with the deaf on a social basis. This book is, therefore, dedicated mainly to you and others like you as you join the growing number of people learning manual communication! Good luck!

Examples of

BASIC HANDSHAPES TO LEARN AND REMEMBER FOR USE
WITH THIS MANUAL

Single Letter Handshapes

Single "A" Handshape

Single Number Handshapes

Single "5" Handshape

Double Letter Handshapes

Double "B" Handshape

Double Number Handshapes

Double "4" Handshape

Open Letter Handshapes

Open "C" Handshape

Flat "0" Handshape

(*Author's Note:* The illustrated handshapes on this page and all other illustrations used in this manual are from the observer's point of view. In other words, the signer's palm or palms face outward.)

In signing, palms may face each other (FEO), face outward toward the observer, face upward, face downward, face inward or toward the body or parts of the body. Once these basic handshapes or positions are understood, the student should have little difficulty in following the written explanations of the sign formations in this manual. Sometimes there are slight variations, but these can always be pointed out by the instructor in charge.

Part I

A Review
of
Fingerspelling
and
Basic Sign Language

"Talk with me."

AN INTRODUCTION TO HELPFUL HINTS AND AIDS
TO BETTER MANUAL COMMUNICATION

Students who have completed a basic course in sign language often feel the need for review in order to develop minimal conversational skills needed to communicate with deaf persons. The author discovered through long teaching experience that among the problems encountered were those dealing with clear and expressive fingerspelling, the use of numbers and figures, and retention of and understanding of subtle differences between groups of signs. These problems were most predominant although the need and desire for an enlarged sign vocabulary was of importance also.

To help overcome fingerspelling problems, a few lessons are offered providing some insight into the key to clear and rhythmic fingerspelling. These exercises are intended basically to give the student and teacher suggestions on how to overcome such problems. Additional exercises can be formulated along the same pattern when and if desired or the same lessons can be used over and over from time to time. The same solution has been offered more or less in helping the student to understand how to communicate numbers, figures, and counting effectively. Illustrations are provided with line explanations which should make clear expression an easy task. These two problems are faced first because they are basic to improved expressive and receptive communication skills beyond the basic course.

Lessons 7 through 18 are designed to enhance the sign vocabulary of the student as well as to give additional practice in the use of the basic signs covered previously. These lessons are categorized around basic themes or subjects which should help the student retain the vocabulary with less difficulty. The plan also should enable the teacher to provide opportunities for informal class discussion or conversation on a specific topic. For example, after studying Lesson 8 which deals with common foods and drink, it should be possible to start a conversation about dinner parties or eating out in restaurants and the like to reinforce the lesson, the practice material, and so on. Such informal conversations in class will tend to make the student more at ease in using signs.

Lesson 19 introduces some of the newer signs for prefixes and suffixes as developed in recent years by the S.E.E. group in California which was mentioned in "Note to the Instructor" on page xii. This is not all-inclusive but rather represents some affixes which have found acceptance among users of sign language in many areas of the nation. Lessons 21 through 29 deal with mixed word groups that frequently have caused students of American Sign Language the most difficulty because basically individual signs traditionally have conveyed specific concepts. The author defines sign language, per se, as an "idea language" for this very reason. This fact makes it possible often to express a precise idea in less "words" than would be needed to say the same thing in English, but it also causes problems for the student who is attempting to express himself adequately in English because he finds that many words carrying the same concept are signed alike or very similarly. Another factor of importance is that dealing with the so-called "new signs." What many people term "new signs" are not actually new; rather they are simply adaptations of existing signs. This is clearly exemplified in groups of signs such as: family, class, group, team, association, etc., all of which convey the idea of a group. Use of the initial letter of these words merely makes the signs more compatible with English and this is good for teaching purposes or even conversational purposes.

Finally the last lesson in this part deals with interpretation of songs and poems into the language of signs. This, too, is intended only to introduce this aspect of signing. Follow-up is left to the teacher.

A REVIEW QUIZ OF BASIC SIGNS

This quiz is based on some of the signs you learned in the beginning-level class. For purposes of testing your memory and fluency in the use of sign language and fingerspelling, take this brief review quiz. Try to sign all underscored words; fingerspell all other words.

1. Which boy did you talk about?

2. Do you know who I saw under the table?

3. What is found among the trees in the forest?

4. "Will you come into my parlor?" said the spider to the fly.

5. Can you jump over the fence?

6. In English, we learn how to write better.

7. My boyfriend told me that he would take me to the beach.

8. Robert did that by himself.

9. I like the poem, "Let me live in a house by the side of the road."

10. You must practice reading signs and fingerspelling by yourselves.

11. Is your home above or below sea level?

12. Some people like to travel by themselves.

13. Who is standing behind that tree?

14. What part of the U.S. do you come from?

15. It is about 40 miles from Washington to Baltimore.

16. That is much more than I can take.

17. Would you please thank him for helping us with this work?

18. Where did you go to school?

19. Do you live in Metropolitan Washington now?

20. When Josephine first arrived here, she felt homesick.

LESSON 1

FINGERSPELLING PROBLEMS

The student who has completed a basic or beginning course in sign language or manual communication often continues to find fingerspelling the most difficult to master or, more pertinently, to read. This is natural and should cause no undue concern because only time and practice in expressive and receptive fingerspelling can enable one to become both a fluent speller and reader. The brief exercises in this lesson are designed to help improve natural and casual fluctuation of the hand and fingers in fingerspelling. This, in turn, will help enable the student to develop the necessary rhythm and transition from one letter to the next for clarity and easy readability.

The key here is to do each of the following exercises rhythmically, gradually increasing speed with each successive practice.

Troublesome Letter Combinations	Double Letters and Formal Names
AEOS	XENIA
DPKT	PLOPPED
BWLZ	MISSISSIPPI
XUAJ	TENNESSEE
VILI	MASSACHUSETTS
EOSO	CALIFORNIA
MNUZ	PENNSYLVANIA
OOPS	OSAWATOMIE
XYIJ	TUSCALOOSA
SCOE	

Phrases

Aesop's Fables	Xenia, Ohio
Dip Stick	a Plopped plume
Blue Waltz	Mississippi Showboat
XOP Sorority	Tennessee Hillbilly
Vigilant Committee	Osawatomie, Kansas

More Phrases

A big blue bird	the Eastover soprano
a deep pink kite	the major new zoo
a black walled log	the old optical style
the ex-Don Juan	the excellent young judge
the vital little link	the scattered cones of Egypt

LESSON 2

FINGERSPELLING EXERCISES

This practice lesson, if followed through and used as a practice outside of class, should help you to develop more clarity, rhythm, and smoothness in your fingerspelling. You can try practicing in front of a mirror to keep check on your own fingerspelling. Speed is NOT essential; fingerspell with more confidence in yourself.

I. **Try this limerick, just for a kick:**

> A tutor who tooted the flute
> Tried to teach two young tooters to toot.
>   Said the two to the tutor
>   "Is it harder to toot or
> To tutor two tooters to toot?
>   ---Wells

How about this little verse, or worse?

> And here's the happy, bounding flea ---
> You cannot tell the he from she.
> The sexes look alike, you see;
> But she can tell, and so can he.
>   ---Young

II. **Try these for fun; don't run them together!**

> tin - sin - thin - shin - chin
> bat - bass - bath - bash - batch
> mat - mass - math - mash - match
> tie - sigh - thigh - shy
> tank - sank - thank - shank
> taw - saw - thaw - Shaw

III. **Some words sound alike, don't they? Important for interpreters!**

> cud - cod - cawed
> done - don - dawn
> tuck - tock - talk
> tut - tot - taught
> cut - cot - caught
> huck - hock - hawk
> fond - fawned - fund
> chalk - chock - chuck
> wrought - rot - rut

LESSON 3

CONTEXTUAL FINGERSPELLING

The following "tongue-twisters", or perhaps we could call them "finger-twisters", were composed by the author for practice in developing rhythm and smooth transition from one letter to the next and from one word to the next. It is important to keep in mind that minute pauses are essential between words, but not between letters within words; otherwise, you may have a "mumbo-jumbo" of run-on words. It is also helpful to develop expression, both on the face and with the fingers, for clarity and meaning. Fingerspelling should not be "flat" or just straight spelling, but rather it should be as expressive as possible. Your instructor can demonsrate expressive fingerspelling and then you can practice it with this exercise.

1. The big blue hat blew over the barn.
2. The tough teacher taught me how to tangle with the trouble.
3. The courteous caller cancelled the call.
4. The mellow mildew marked the mall.
5. The priceless platter plopped to the floor.
6. A fat fly flew past the fiddlestick fast.
7. Lady Luck loves lovely lilacs.
8. The mean, merciless master moaned for his mutt.
9. The silent sisters stuttered senselessly.
10. The zealous zebra zoomed past the zombie.

Some well-known quotations and current quotes were selected for this practice lesson in fingerspelling. The objective of the lesson is to give you continued practice in developing rhythm and smooth transition which are vital to clear and effective fingerspelling. In addition, it is suggested that you try putting expression into your spelling as well as on your face.

1. "The wolf also shall dwell with the lamb, and the leopard shall lie down with the kid."

2. "Many are called, but few are chosen."

3. "A decision will have to be gained by waiting, for every day the enemy becomes stronger."

4. "He did not have any idea of retiring, nor could we persuade him, even to take a vacation."

5. "Some teachers can really help a dullard, but bright students often seem to learn little from them."

6. "The atomic fission weapons have created nervous tension throughout the world."

7. "Because of your slight effort in your studies, you will undoubtedly fail."

8. "And now abideth faith, hope, charity."

9. "If the blind lead the blind, both shall fall into the ditch."

10. "The winter is past, the rain is over and gone, the flowers appear on the earth; the time of the singing of the birds is come and the voice of the turtle is heard in our land."

Additional Suggestion:
You might try signing these thoughts when you have completed the finger-spelling practice.

PRACTICE TEST 1

Lessons 1 - 2 - 3

This Practice Test is for **fingerspelling** only. Try to fingerspell each word as you say it aloud. Be sure your letters are clear and smooth and not jerky or bumpy. Follow the basic principle of spelling in syllables. You may take this test over and over using a mirror to see yourself if you like.

I. **Interesting Facts from Here and There:**

1. The Mississippi River is America's largest.

2. There is a town in Missouri called California.

3. Louisiana is another Missouri town.

4. The Schuylkill River runs through Philadelphia.

5. Kanorado is a town on the Kansas-Colorado border.

6. My hometown is Peabody, Kansas.

7. Peabody Street and Kansas Avenue intersect in N.W. Washington.

8. Yellowstone National Park is located in Wyoming.

9. The world's longest bridge lies across Lake Pontchartrain near New Orleans.

10. Many hill people live in Arkansas and Tennessee.

II. **Quotable Quotes from the Author:**

11. The peculiar pumpkin peered through the potato patch.

12. The ghastly ghost gloated gaily with glee.

13. The timid tiger trampled through the thistle.

14. The jazzy jackal jigged around the janitor.

15. The dazed donkey danced down the dock.

16. The lazy loafer liked to lick licorice lollipops.

17. The flashy fish floated freely through the foam.

18. The stingy stewardess slowly stirred the stew.

19. The hairy hoarder hoarded away the hair.

20. The arrogant associate argued around the author.

9

LESSON 4

TIME WORDS AND PHRASES

In this lesson, you will find a review of time words and phrases which the Intermediate student should be able to sign clearly and fluently. Check yourself by going through the list to see if you are able to do this.

8 o'clock — Sign: "time 8".

7:45 p.m. — Sign: "7-45-p.m."

later — Use the "L" handshape on R hand; place thumb on L palm; move forward.

in a minute, moment — Use the "1" handshape; same position as "later"; move slightly forward very quickly.

next (in time) — Use Dbl. "closed-5" handshape on L hand, palm facing you and R hand above and slightly in front of L. Move R hand fingers over L and come to rest at back.

next (in line) — Use "5" handshape on L hand, palm towards you, and "L" on R with thumb slightly towards you; move "L" out from one finger to another so that thumb points towards the next person or thing.

morning, noon, afternoon, evening, night — Right hand and arm represents the sun and its position in the sky; left hand rests inside bend for morning and at elbow for noon and afternoon moving toward right hand for night.

all morning, all afternoon, all day, all evening, all night — The same pattern of signs exists here, also. For example, make the sign for morning and move R hand up to noon position, keeping L hand inside bend of R arm. The only exception is for "all night" which requires an "underneath" sweep of the R hand and arm, just the opposite of "all day".

today — Sign: "now" + "day".

tonight — Sign: "now" + "night".

this morning — Sign: "now" + "morning".

this afternoon — Sign: "now" + "afternoon".

this evening — Sign: "now" + "evening".

yesterday — Use the R thumb, nail on cheek, move one jump up and back to indicate past time.

the day before yesterday or the other day or two days ago — Use the same initial position and movement as above, but raise index finger as you move up and back.

10

three days ago — Use the same initial position and movement as above, but raise index and middle finger as you move up and back.

tomorrow — Use R thumb, positioned on cheek with thumb pointing back; move forward in a semi-circle on cheek to indicate time ahead.

the day after tomorrow or two days from now — Use the same initial position and movement, but raise index finger as you move forward.

three days from now — Use the same initial position and movement but raise index and middle fingers as you move forward.

this week, this month, this year — <u>Sign</u>: "now" + "week"; "now" + "month"; "now" + "year".

last week, last month, last year — <u>Sign</u>: "past" + "week"; "past" + "month"; "past" + "year".
[Note: for "last week" and "last year", we have abbreviated forms. Last week is signed "week" (with palm facing you) + "past", keeping the "1" handshape. Last year is signed with the dbl. "1" handshape, palms facing you with wrists crossed; move "1"s back simultaneously towards past.]

one week ago — <u>Sign</u>: "one" + "week" + "past" or the same as "last week".

next week — <u>Sign</u>: "week" but move "1" ahead in a semicircle after "week".

two weeks from now — <u>Sign</u>: "week" as in "next week" using "2" handshape.

next month — <u>Sign</u>: "next" + "month".

next year — <u>Sign</u>: "next" + "year" or use abbreviated form by placing R "S" on top of L "S" as at the end of the sign "year"; move R hand out ahead in semicircle, opening to "1" handshape with a flicking motion.

two years from now — <u>Sign</u> literally or as above in abbreviated form, but opening up to a "2".

every week, weekly — <u>Sign</u>: "week" repeatedly 3 or 4 times.

every month, monthly — <u>Sign</u>: "month" repeatedly 3 or 4 times.

every year, annually, yearly — <u>Sign</u>: abbreviated form of "next year", repeating rapidly a couple of times.

every two years, biennally — <u>Sign</u>: as above but using "2" handshape.

often — Use dbl. open "B" handshape with L hand palm up; bring R hand down on L, fingers touching base of palm; move forward in one jump.

11

frequently — <u>Sign</u>: "often" in rapid succession.

over and over — <u>Sign</u>: "again" and "again".

sometimes — use open "B" handshape on L hand, palm up and "1" handshape on R hand; strike L palm with R "1" two times moderately.

occasionally, once in a while, seldom — <u>Sign</u>: "sometimes" at progressively slower pace.

every so often, every now and then — Use "5" handshape on L hand, palm facing right and open "B" handshape on R hand; move R hand in short jumps alternating between fingers of L hand.

every Monday, every Tuesday, etc. — <u>Sign</u>: "Monday" or "Tuesday" without circular motion; simply move the "M" or "T" down to indicate successive Mondays or Tuesdays.

after — Use dbl. open "B" handshape, palms facing you; place R hand outside and adjacent to L and move out.

before — Same position as above, but place R hand inside L and move back towards yourself.

once, twice, thrice, four times, five times — All of these are made with the L palm open and facing upward; with R hand, strike a "1" against the L palm in a sweeping motion once. For twice use "2", etc.

previous — <u>Sign</u>: "past".

previously — <u>Sign</u>: "past" two times.

just (meaning very recently), just a while ago, just a minute ago — Use "X" handshape against cheek with index finger pointed back; slightly "scratch" cheek in this position.

always — Use "1" handshape; move in continuous circle.

forever — <u>Sign</u>: "for" + "always".

never — Use open "B" handshape, palm facing left; move down in zig-zag fashion.

first — Use "1" on R hand; bring back against L thumb.

last — Use "1" on R hand; bring down against little finger.

weekdays — <u>Sign</u>: "week" + "days".

weekend — <u>Sign</u>: "week" + "end" or "complete".

since that time, **all along, up** to **now, ever,** several times (**been**) now — For the underscored words in this group, use Sign for "been" which is the dbl. "1" handshape, fingers pointing at each other over back of R shoulder; move forward in an almost complete circle.

hour — Use "1" handshape against L open palm; move around clockwise.

minute — Sign as in "hour" but move index finger briefly and briskly once as a minute moves on the hour hand.

second — Sign as above but with much briefer movement.

in a half hour — Sign: "hour" preceded by "1/2".

EXERCISE 1

Sign the following sentences, giving particular attention to the **boldface** words or phrases; fingerspell all words which cannot or should not be signed.

1. It is **now 8 o'clock**.

2. It was **7:45 p.m.** when you came in.

3. I will go there **later**.

4. I will be with you **in a minute**.

5. **Next** time you come, please bring your materials.·

6. Wasn't that a beautiful **morning**?

7. Mary will meet John at **noon**.

8. Jane will be home this **evening**.

9. At **night** Joanne's dog barks.

10. It rained **all morning** and **all afternoon** today.

11. It snowed **all day** last Friday.

12. My mother waited up for him **all night** last night.

13. **Yesterday** Mary went to the dentist's office.

14. **This morning** I was late for classes.

15. I am going on a trip **this afternoon**.

16. **Tonight** we are going to the theatre.

17. I will finish paying for my car **this month**.

18. Hurricane Agnes flooded many areas **last week**.

19. **Five years ago** Pete received his college degree.

20. Will is planning to go to Europe **next year**.

21. **Two weeks from now** will be the start of my vacation.

22. Some people go to Florida **every year**.

EXERCISE 2

Sign the following sentences, giving particular attention to the **boldface** words or phrases; fingerspell all words which cannot or should not be signed.

1. **Sometimes** I go to the movies by myself.

2. Bob **seldom** eats breakfast.

3. Tom **often** wanders into the woods for solitude.

4. Donna **frequently** misses her 8 o'clock class.

5. I keep telling him **over and over** not to do that.

6. **Never** say you can't do something.

7. **Every now and then** Mary gets a bad cold.

8. He called **just a while ago**.

9. I'm **always** interested in a good recipe.

10. The **first** person in line is the team captain.

11. I look forward to the **weekends** and dread the **weekdays**.

12. He arrived **after** the bus had gone.

13. Have you seen me **before**?

14. He spoke of a **previous** letter to you.

15. **Since that time** many changes have been made.

16. **Up to now** Dick has not heard from Donna.

17. Have you **ever** stopped to ponder that question?

18. Her car has broken down **several times now.**

19. Ten **seconds** is 1/6 of one **minute.**

20. **In a half hour**, I will be through.

21. **Every Sunday** we have an early dinner.

22. I want to see you **again** in **a couple of days.**

LESSON 5

REVIEW OF MONEY SIGNS

Since a lot of daily conversation is concerned with money, how much something costs, how much one paid for something, and the rising cost of living in general, a review of "money signs" should be beneficial.

a penny-1¢ — index finger on R temple; bring out.

a nickel-5¢ — "5" handshape on R temple; bring out.

a dime-10¢ — index finger on R temple with thumb out; bring out to "10".

a quarter-25¢ — "25" handshape with back tip of index finger on R temple; bring out.

a half-dollar-50¢ — "5" handshape with back tip of index finger on R temple; bring out to "50".

a dollar-$1.00 — "1" handshape; twist arm & finger in a short semi-circle.

a dollar bill — Sign "1"; then with the left hand open to a "B" handshape, palm facing right, grasp the left hand next to the thumb and slide out.

For all of the figures listed here, use the number (1,2,3, etc.); handshape; twist arm and finger in a short, sharp semi-circle.

$1.00	$5.00	$9.00—After $9.00, one
2.00	6.00	must sign the figure or
3.00	7.00	number plus the "dollar
4.00	8.00	bill" sign . . . e.g. "10" +
		"dollar bill"

Dollars and cents may be signed: $3.00   25; <u>Or</u> 3.00 and 25¢ (rare); <u>Or</u> 3 point (.) 25

For Practice

$ 1.50	$ 695.00	$ 25,995
3.25	125.50	15,695
10.50	1,525.00	1,364,287
5.99	250.95	125,000

EXERCISES

Sign the following sentences, giving particular attention to the **boldface** words or figures; fingerspell all words which cannot or should not be signed.

1. In the old days, a newspaper used to cost a **penny**.

2. It used to cost a **nickel** for a candy bar.

3. Now it costs a **dime** for a pack of gum.

4. A short taxi ride costs more than a **quarter**.

5. The profile of JFK is on new **half-dollar** coins.

6. What is the value of the **dollar** at present?

7. Whose face is on a **one dollar bill**?

8. A subscription to the Washington Post used to be **$3.25**.

9. Yogart usually costs around **41¢** per cup.

10. Few people have won the **$64,000** question!

11. The plane fare from New York to Los Angeles is **$250.95** round trip.

12. It cost **$3,000,000.00** for that airfield to be built.

13. One bar of soap can easily cost **27¢** today.

14. That fabulous mobile home I saw in Ocean City costs **$15,695**.

15. Most suburban homes cost **$18,000** or more!

16. That blouse costs **$6.98** plus tax.

17. Our new color TV set cost my father **$495.75**.

18. My son's new pants cost me **$8.50**.

19. I went to the horse races and won **$16.78!!!**

20. When you add **27,689** and **32,523** you get **60,212**.

NUMBERS, FIGURES, AND COUNTING

In American Sign Language, it is possible to count up to 999 on *one* hand! However, there are a few certain basic "rules" to follow in the formation of numbers manually. Mainly, these are to insure *clarity*. Once you get to 30 without any difficulty, you will have no trouble going on to an indefinite number or figure.

One   Two   Three   Four   Five

Six   Seven   Eight   Nine   Ten

Eleven   Twelve   Thirteen   Fourteen   Fifteen

Sixteen   Seventeen   Eighteen   Nineteen   Twenty

Twenty-one   Twenty-three   Twenty-four   Twenty-five

18

ALL double digits of the same number are formed in the same way, as illustrated below:

Twenty-two

Thirty-three

Sixty-six

One exception to this point would be with the numbers 66, 77, 88, and 99. There is a short, quick break made between them. E.G the "6" handshape opens and then comes down to another "6" for sixty-six.

The hundreds are indicated by the number followed by the "C" handshape. (*C* is the Roman numeral for hundred.)

One hundred

Three hundred

The thousands are indicated by the number followed by the "M" handshape brought down against the opposite hand, palm open and facing upward as illustrated below:

For *million,* the "M" movement is repeated once, striking the palm, moving up and striking down again. For *billion,* repeat movement twice.

To the right is the illustration for the sign for "twice". It is made by the "2" handshape swept down on the opposite palm and brought up again in one movement. The signs for "once", and "thrice" or "3 times" are made in the same way with the numbers "1" and "3". 4 times and 5 times may be done likewise, but after that, it is necessary to say "6" and then "time" and so forth.

In the 60's, 70's, 80's, and 90's, there is a subtle point to remember and follow, especially for clarity or to avoid confusion. This is when one digit is larger or smaller than the other as in: 67, 68, 69 or 76, 78, 79 or 86, 87, 89 and 96, 97, 98. When the smaller digit is *first* the hand position is slightly downward to the right and moves up left to the larger digit as in 67, 68, and 69. (Illustrated with arrows at *top,* from the observer's point of view.) When the first digit is *larger* than the second, the hand position is straight up and drops down slightly to the right to the smaller digit as in 76, 86, 96, etc. (Illustrated with arrows at bottom.) Once you have mastered this subtle point, you will have no difficulty making these numbers *clearly.*

67

68

69

76

78

79

86

87

89

96

97

98

Telephone numbers and *years* are made or formed the way they are spoken.

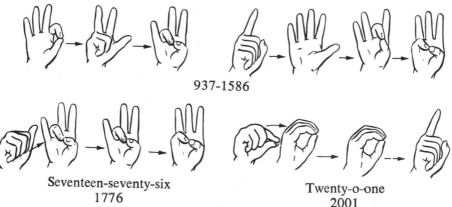

937-1586

Seventeen-seventy-six
1776

Twenty-o-one
2001

Addresses are formed the way they are spoken: Ex. If you live at 6913 Southern Ave., you would say "69-13" and then fingerspell "Southern Ave."

Fractions are formed the way they are written symbolically. Simply form the numerator and then drop the hand down to the denominator.

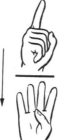

One fourth

Five eighths

Percentages are formed by the number, followed by the percent sign (%), which would be the "Flat 0" handshape moved in the same way the written symbol is made, as illustrated below:

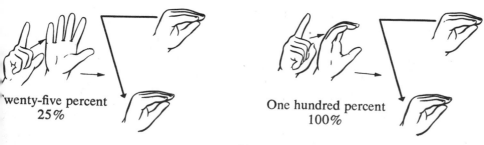

Twenty-five percent
25%

One hundred percent
100%

LESSON 6

REVIEW OF NUMBERS AND COUNTING

Included in this Review are numbers, figures, years, fractions and percentages. You should be able to go through this list and sign each one without difficulty. The review of numbers and figures preceding this list should help you. Practice until you are able to do them fluently.

Numbers and Figures

			Years
67	99	1,301	1968
86	111	1,666	1674
98	156	4,541	1514
31	169	8,676	1920
25	188	15,335	1981
55	354	25,405	1967
74	396	50,681	1970
13	570	99,989	2015
16	944	5,063,261	1776
11	765	56,787,543	1492

Addresses / Fractions / Percents

Addresses	Fractions	Percents
789 Central Avenue	4/5	25%
1936 Main Street	7/8	50
8795 Willow Street	3/16	33
4815 Wesley Blvd.	11/32	18
2329 Pocahontas Court	9/64	100
10 Downing Street	3/8	125

EXERCISES

Sign the following sentences, giving particular attention to the **boldface** words or figures; fingerspell all words which cannot or should not be signed.

1. I can easily remember my mother's age because she was born in **1900**.

2. Our telephone number is **927-1670**, in case you want to call us.

3. Most American cars cost between **2,500** and **6,000** dollars.

4. Would you spend **$369.99** for a fur coat?

5. The invitation is for Sunday, February **19, 1972**, from **3 to 4** p.m.

6. So far there are **354** people living in the new town of Hilton.

7. Recent evidence shows America was discovered before **1492**.

8. The home of the Mayor of Hilton cost **$50,681.99**.

9. How much is **3/16** and **7/8**?

10. Less than **75 percent** of all registered voters will vote.

11. My address is **6017 Mustang Court**, Riverdale, Maryland **20840**.

12. Don't you often wonder what **1984** will be like in Washington?

13. What would you do if you won a **$500.00** contest?

14. What is the sum of **25,574** and **3,689**?

15. How old will you be in the year **1980**?

16. The population of Belair at Bowie is now approaching **35,000**.

17. Many people here will remember the **1972** floods of Hurricane Agnes.

18. **Forty-five percent** of the new midget cars were defective.

19. Over **250,000** persons were left homeless in this summer's floods.

20. We must cut this board to **5 and 9/16** inches.

PRACTICE TEST 2

Lessons 4 - 5 - 6

Go through this practice test without referring back to the last three lessons to see how many of the **boldface** words you can remember the signs for. After you have gone through the test go back over the lessons to check yourself.

1. Churchill's **address** was 10 Downing Street in London for **many years**.

2. **Next year** I hope to save **$250.00**.

3. The telephone numbers for my office are **447-0835** or TTY **447-0885**.

4. What would you do **this week** if you won **$1,525,000.00**?

5. **Yesterday** it rained about **4/5** of an inch.

6. Bill lost **$10.75** in bets **last month**.

7. Jane was so sick, she threw up **five times** during **the night**.

8. What will **1981** be like if **1972** is like this?

9. I counted **1,666** sheep **last night** but still couldn't sleep.

10. I woke up at **3:45 this morning** and got up to write this test.

11. **Sometimes** it's hard to imagine what **forever** really means.

12. We may get a **foot** of snow **next winter**.

13. It seems like it has rained about **60%** of the time **this summer**.

14. The address you are looking for is **8420** Pocahontas Drive.

15. How much is **8,786** and **5,467**?

16. **Every week** we must figure the **percentage** of our income that goes to taxes.

17. The boat costs **$899.95** on sale; **later** it will be **$1,195.00**.

18. **Two weeks from now** will be my **43rd** birthday.

19. **A week ago**, we spent **$38.97** on groceries alone!

20. That store is at **308** Division Street; the phone number is **827-9161**.

21. We **seldom** go away for a full **weekend**.

22. **Previously** I thought every **hour** had **60 minutes**, now I am not so sure!

AUTOMOBILES, PARKING AND TRAFFIC

"Park here, please!"

Automobiles:

The names of most cars are fingerspelled but a few are abbreviated like "Chev.", "Olds", and "V.W."

The "Big 3" of American automobiles have initial letter signs as follows:

Imperial "I"
Cadillac "C"
Lincoln "L"
    On the shoulder move upward in two forward circular motions.

In talking about "parking your car" or "moving your car" or "stopping your car", use the "3" handshape to represent your car and the palm of the other hand to represent the place where you park or stop <u>or</u> to represent the roof of the garage or carport. Move the "3" (your car) according to the action indicated in phrases like below:

park (your car)
parking lot.
parking ticket
put the car in the garage (or carport)
back up - back out
pull over
move up
park here
park near the street (house, store)

skid — <u>Mime</u> <u>sign</u> the act of skidding, using the "3" handshape.

come to a sudden stop — <u>Mime</u> <u>sign</u> the act of stopping suddenly, using the "3" handshape.

The sign for traffic is made using both hands in the double-5 handshape, with palms facing each other upright and moving the hands alternately back and forth against each other rapidly. Use this sign in expressions such as:

heavy traffic   **light traffic**
slow traffic   **traffic ticket**

For a term like "traffic jam", sign traffic first, followed by the sign for stuck OR by using the dble. "3" handshape and indicating a line of cars by backing up one hand from the other.

EXERCISES

Sign the following sentences, giving particular attention to the **boldface** words; fingerspell all words which cannot or should not be signed.

1. A **Cadillac** is a very expensive car.

2. Some people prefer **Lincolns**.

3. I think the **Imperial** is a beautiful car.

4. **Park** your car at the end of the drive-way.

5. An inexpensive **parking lot** is hard to find in D.C.

6. I was parked on the wrong side of the street so I got a **parking ticket**.

7. Because it is going to snow, I **put** the car **in the garage**.

8. **Back** the car **out** of the garage, please.

9. Will you **pull over** and let me out here?

10. In **heavy traffic**, one **moves up** very slowly.

11. **Park here** so we are close to the store.

12. If you will **park** the truck **near** the **store** entrance, it will be much easier to load.

13. Cars frequently **skid** on icy roads.

14. Because of the accident, all traffic **came to a sudden stop**.

15. The rain caused **traffic to be slow**.

16. That was **light traffic** for the normal rush hour!

17. My **V.W.** has not been working lately.

18. **Chevrolets** are good cars. (sign "Chev.")

19. 1956 **Olds.** were big, heavy cars.

20. Some small towns seem to "give away" **traffic tickets**!

LESSON 8

COMMON FOODS AND DRINKS

"I love hamburgers!"

MEATS

meat — Use dbl. "5" handshape; with R index finger and thumb; grasp L hand between index finger and thumb; gently squeeze L hand two or three times.

chicken — <u>Mime Sign</u>: Closed "G" handshape at lips; move as a chicken would in opening and closing its beak.

hamburgers — <u>Mime Sign</u>: Clasping hands together, move as you would in making hamburger patties.

hot dogs — <u>Mime Sign</u>: Use dbl. "G" handshape, G's pointing toward and touching each other; move out to indicate links.

sausage — <u>Mime Sign</u>: Use dbl. "S" handshape side by side; open and close hands as you move out to indicate making links.

turkey — Use "G" handshape pointing down from chin; shake hand as you move down and out. This represents the turkey's "tie".

duck or goose — <u>Sign</u>: "no, no" at or under chin; this mimics a duck or goose quacking.

28

fish — Mime Sign: Use the open "B" handshape with fingers placed at R pulse; weave hand forward like a fish swimming.

shrimp, crab, lobster — Mime Sign: Using the dbl. "V" handshape pointing outward, mimic one of these opening and closing its pincers, like in cutting something with scissors; hold hands close together for shrimp, a little farther apart for crab, and even farther apart for lobster.

oysters — Mime Sign: Use flat "O" handshape on L hand with opening slightly up; place fingers of R hand into opening and move back and forth. This represents an oyster in a shell.

rabbit — Mime Sign: Use dbl. "U" handshape above ears; wiggle back and forth like rabbit ears.

bacon — Mime Sign: Use dbl. "U" handshape with palms facing downward and one "U" touching the other; move out R hand in the shape of crisp bacon.

VEGETABLES

vegetables — Use abbreviation "veg".

potatoes — Mime Sign: Use crooked "V" handshape on R hand; tap the back of left hand two or three times. [This represents checking to see if the potato is cooked.]

corn — Mime Sign: With L index finger pointing outward, mime the shelling of corn from the cob with your R thumb and index finger representing the knife.

corn-on-the-cob — Mime Sign: Eating corn-on-the-cob.

beans — Mime Sign: With L index finger pointing outward to represent the bean pod, pick the bean seeds in three movements.

string beans — Indicate with index fingers and thumbs a single string bean, followed by the sign for "beans" as explained above.

lettuce — Use curved open "B" handshape to represent a leaf of lettuce; tap bottom of palm on head just above temple.

cabbage — Sign like lettuce but use the open "A" handshape; the difference is that cabbage leaves are more closely formed than lettuce leaves.

onions — Use "X" handshape at temple just outside the eye; twist hand back and forth.

peas — Use dbl. "G" handshape, with G's touching each other; move R "G" out quickly picking the peas from the pod.

tomatoes — Use dbl. "1" with R "1" at lips to indicate "red"; strike tip of L "1" to indicate slicing action.

carrots — Mime Sign: eating a carrot stick.

Spinach, beets and certain other vegetables at present have no sign.

MILK PRODUCTS

milk — Mime Sign: Use "C" handshape as in holding a cow's teat in milking; close to an "S" several times to indicate milking action. [To talk about milking a cow, simply use both hands.]

cream — Mime Sign: Use "C" handshape on R hand; place on open L palm and move as in skimming cream from the top of a pail of milk.

ice cream — Mime Sign: With fist closed as in holding an ice cream cone, move "cone" as you would in licking the ice cream.

cheese — Use dbl. "5" handshape with base of palms pressed together, one on top of the other;twist R hand back and forth in a pressing motion.

butter — Mime Sign: With the "U" handshape on the R hand representing a knife and the L palm representing a slice of bread, go through the motion of spreading butter in two strokes.

sour cream — Sign: "sour" as in bitter and "cream".

DRINKS AND OTHER LIQUIDS

water — Use "W" handshape with index finger touching lips; move out and back to lips two or three times quickly.

coffee — Mime Sign: Grinding coffee with one "S" handshape on top of the other; move top hand in a grinding motion.

tea — Mime Sign: Use the "O" handshape on L hand positioned like a small cup; use the "F" handshape on the R hand to indicate holding a tea bag; dip and stir "tea bag" in the "cup".

wine — Use "W" handshape flush against R cheek; move in circles.

whiskey (liquor) — With index fingers and little finger out on both hands; place R hand on back of the L hand and move R hand up and down twice.

beer — Use "B" handshape at R edge of mouth; move down slightly a couple of times. [This sign is almost like brown which is made with a larger sweeping motion.]

vinegar — Use "V" handshape on lips; Sign like "water".

vanilla — Use "V" handshape; hold hand slightly out and shake back and forth sidewise.

OTHER FOODS

bread — Use dbl. open "B" handshape with L palm down and fingers pointing right; move fingers of R hand over back of the L hand in a slicing motion, starting at base of thumb.

sandwich — Use dbl. open "B" handshape, R palm on L palm; turn fingers towards mouth and move hands as in clapping very lightly.

toast — 1) Use crooked "V" handshape on R hand and "5" handshape on L hand, palm facing right; letting the "V" represent a fork, touch the hand on both the palm and back.

2) For a drink "toast", simply Mime Sign the act of raising a glass or drink in toast, using both hands and bringing them nearly together.

cake — Use "C" handshape on R hand and open "B" on the L, palm upward; move "C" with fingers and thumb touching the L palm in a twisting motion to the right.

cookies — Sign like "cake" but repeat movement several times to indicate act of cutting cookies.

crackers — Use "S" handshape on R hand; hit L elbow two times.

pie — Mime Sign: Cutting a piece of pie, represented by open "B" handshape on the L hand, palm up, with the open "B" handshape on the R.

dressing — Sign "dress" in 2 or 3 rapidly repeated movements.

soup — Use "U" handshape on R hand and open "B" on L hand, palm up to represent bowl; Mime Sign act of eating soup.

eggs — Use dbl. "U" handshape, fingers pointed outward; place R "U" over L and mime sign the breaking of an egg.

scrambled eggs — Sign: "mixed up" + "eggs".

hard-boiled eggs — Sign: "hard" + "boiled" + "eggs". [Sign for "boiled" is made by holding L hand, palm down, and making sign for "fire" with R hand under it. Move in circular motion.]

soft-boiled eggs — Sign: "soft" + "boiled" + "eggs".

fried eggs — Sign: "cook" for "fried" + "eggs".

31

jelly or jam — Use "J" handshape in a sweeping motion over upturned L palm.

gravy — Sign like "cream" but continue circular movements as in stirring gravy. [In the South, "gravy" is signed like "grease" or "fat" by gripping hand below little finger with R index finger and thumb and sliding off two or three times.

syrup — Use R index finger; "wipe" R edge of mouth to indicate wiping dripping syrup from mouth.

chocolate — Sometimes abbreviated "choc". Sign is made using "C" on R hand, placing R hand on back of L hand and moving in complete circles two or three times. [Note: If "C" is moved back and forth over back of L hand instead of in circles, it means "dirty" or "filthy".]

salad dressing — Spell "salad"; Sign: "dressing".

mayonnaise — Use "Y" handshape on R hand; place on back of L hand and wiggle or waddle in a spreading motion toward L wrist.

salt — Use slightly open dbl. "U" handshape, palms facing downward; place R "U" over L and alternately move fingers up and down a few times.

pepper — Use "F" handshape on R hand; position hand near R side of forehead and shake.

sugar — Use open "B" handshape; move over lips twice [Don't confuse this sign with "sweet" which is made the same except over chin rather than lips.]

candy — Use "U" handshape; move over lips twice as in "sugar". [Don't confuse this sign with "cute" which is made the same except over the chin rather than lips].

FRUIT

dessert — Use dbl. "D" handshape, palms facing each other; bring "D's" together twice.

apples — Use "X" handshape on R hand; place against R cheek and twist back and forth.

peaches — Use open "B" handshape; with fingers on R cheek and thumb under jaw, move down twice bringing fingers and thumb together to represent the fuzzy skin of the peach.

pears — Use the flat "O" handshape on the L hand, fingers pointing right; grasp whole fist with R hand, finger on fingers, and slide back off L hand; then let fingers meet fingers. [This denotes the shape of a pear.]

cherries — Sign: "Red" followed by grasping the L little finger with the tips of the R thumb index and middle fingers and moving clockwise two or three times.

grapes — <u>Mime Sign</u>: Use the crooked "5" handshape on R hand; let L hand hang down and place R fingers on back of L hand. Move up and down to represent a cluster of grapes.

oranges — <u>Mime Sign</u>: Use the "C" handshape in front of mouth; squeeze hand twice as you would in squeezing juice from an orange.

watermelon — <u>Sign</u>: "Water" followed by tapping the back of L hand with flick of R middle finger under R thumb as in tapping a melon to test it.

pumpkin — <u>Sign</u> the same way you test a melon.

coconut — <u>Mime Sign</u>: Use the dbl. "C" handshape, fingers pointing at each other; position near ear and shake as you would in checking a coconut for milk.

bananas — <u>Mime Sign</u>: Use "1" handshape on L hand to represent the banana; with R hand mime sign the peeling of a banana.

strawberries — Use the "9" or "F" handshape in front of mouth as in holding a strawberry; pull down and back a couple times as in pulling the stem from the berry when you eat it.

blueberry — <u>Sign</u>: "Blue" and spell "berry" or sign "berry" as in "cherry" but without "red".

blackberry — <u>Sign</u>: "Black" plus above description for "berry".

jello — Use the dbl. "5" handshape, fingers pointing out and palms down; shake hands forward and backwards to imitate the movement of jello when shook.

Sign the following sentences, giving particular attention to the **boldface** words or terms, fingerspell all words which cannot or should not be signed.

1. We had **sausage** and **scrambled eggs** for breakfast.

2. Which do you like better — **clam** chowder or **oyster** stew?

3. Homemade **peach ice cream** is one of my favorite **desserts**.

4. I love **sour cream** on baked **potatoes**.

5. We need more **mayonnaise** and lunch **meat**.

6. The Senate cafeteria is famous for its navy **bean soup**.

7. We plan to have **hamburgers** and **hot dogs** for the cookout.

8. Roast **duck** is a real delicacy if cooked in **wine**.

9. Maryland is noted for its **crab** cakes and **clam** bakes.

10. My folks used to have a very nice **strawberry** patch.

11. Would you like your **sandwich** on **toasted bread**?

12. Have you read the novel "**Coffee, Tea** or Me"?

13. I like **vanilla** milk shakes better than **chocolate** ones.

14. Please pass the **salt** and **pepper**.

15. Some Louisianans go to Florida each year to pick their own **oranges** and grapefruits.

16. Do you like to eat **shrimp** cocktail?

17. **Blueberry** muffins are most delicious.

18. In the summertime, many people love to eat **watermelon**.

19. Liver **gravy** is best when made with **milk**, not **water**.

20. Everyone in my family loves **corn-on-the-cob**.

21. Do we have any **whiskey** left?

22. The Rathskellar sells only two brands of **beer**.

EXERCISE 2

Sign the following sentences, giving particular attention to the **boldface** words or terms; fingerspell all words which cannot or should not be signed.

1. Easter **eggs** are really dyed **hard-boiled eggs**.

2. I eat **soft-boiled eggs** over toast when I am sick.

3. Roast **turkey** stuffed with **oyster dressing** is delicious.

4. Broiled **lobster** is a great seafood, but it is expensive.

5. There are so many different **cheeses** to choose from in most stores.

6. Please buy more **butter** and **cream**.

7. A **fish** fry is usually a lot of fun.

8. We have a large **apple** tree but our **cherry** tree died.

9. **Pumpkin pie** is very good, but filling.

10. I love both **blackberry jam** and **grape jelly**.

11. **Peas** and tiny **onions** are good when cooked together.

12. How do you like your **chicken** — Fried, roasted, broiled or baked?

13. When I was a boy on the farm, we used to eat fried **rabbit**.

14. **Lettuce** and **tomatoes** are basic salad ingredients.

15. Cole slaw is made from shredded **cabbage** and **carrots**.

16. Would you like some **cake** or **cookies** with your tea?

17. **Bananas** are good with **jello** or breakfast cereal.

18. We need some **vinegar** for the salad.

19. My mother always cans some **peaches** and **pears** each summer.

20. **Crackers** and **cheese** make a good appetizer.

21. My wife loves **coconut cream pie**.

22. Be sure to get some **sugar**, and **syrup** on the way home.

35

LESSON 9

AROUND HOME

FAMILIAR SIGNS FOR THE HOME

home — <u>Sign</u>: actually an abbreviated combination of "eat" + "sleep".

house — <u>Mime Sign</u>: Use the "open-B" handshape; fingers touching to represent a roof; move down separating hands.

apartment — Use abbreviation "apt".

foyer — <u>Sign</u>: "entrance" as in enter but with 2 movements.

parlor/living room — Use "L" handshape against chest; strike upwards twice and then sign "room".

dining room — <u>Sign</u>: "eat" using the "D" handshape, followed by "room".

bathroom — <u>Sign</u>: "bath" + "room".

powder room — <u>Sign</u> literally, patting side of face to indicate powdering; follow by "room".

toilet — Use "T" handshape, holding hand out slightly, move "T" briskly back and forth sidewise.

lavatory — <u>Sign</u>: "toilet" or spell out.

bedroom — <u>Sign</u>: "sleep" + "room".

recreation room — Use abbreviation "rec." + "room".

den — Commonly fingerspelled.

kitchen — Use "K" handshape holding hand slightly outward; move "K" briskly back and forth sidewise.

laundry — <u>Sign</u>: "wash" as in washing clothes, or "wash" + "room".

patio — Generally fingerspelled.

garage/carport — Use "3" handshape on the R hand, symbolizing a car; form a roof or cover with L hand; move the "car" in under the roof or cover twice.

furniture — Use "F" handshape holding hand slightly outward; move "F" briskly back and forth sidewise.

closets — Sign: "doors" and Mime Sign "hangers" hanging on a rod. [Use L index Finger for the rod and R index finger to indicate the hangers.]

TABLE ITEMS

plate — Use "open-8" handshape; form the shape of a plate with middle fingers and thumbs. [Movement may change to indicate size.]

glass — Use index finger to tap teeth, representing glass, then mime sign the shape of a glass by cupping R hand in L palm and moving upward.

cup — Mime Sign: forming the shape of a cup as in glass; move slightly up and down twice.

napkin — Mime Sign: Using the "A" handshape, wipe mouth two times.

knife — Use both index fingers; strike R index finger against left index finger; moving sharply out to indicate the sharpness of the knife.

fork — Use "2" handshape on R hand; resting on open L palm; move once to indicate putting fork into something.

spoon — Use "U" handshape; mime sign spooning soup or something.

silverware — Sign: "knives, forks, and spoons" or spell the word.

EXERCISES

Sign the following sentences, giving particular attention to the **boldface** words; fingerspell all words which cannot or should not be signed.

1. Do you live in a **house** or an **apartment**?

2. A **foyer** is nice to have because it gives some privacy.

3. Many **homes** today are being built with both a **dining room** and a **family room**.

4. I wish my **house** had an extra **bathroom** or **powder room**.

5. We hope to remodel our **kitchen** and **bathroom** sometime soon.

6. My wife selected French provincial for our **living** and **dining rooms**.

7. About two years ago we finished building a large **patio** at **home**.

8. Our **laundry room** is a comfortably-sized room.

9. Does your house have a **den** or **recreation room**?

10. What kind or style of **furniture** do you prefer?

11. Not many homes have **garages** in this area.

12. Did you find out why your **toilet** was leaking?

13. Will you please set the **glasses** on the table for me?

14. Our **silverware** is of the "Lily of the Valley" pattern.

15. We need some new coffee **cups** as the old ones are cracked.

16. Where are the dinner **napkins** you ironed last night?

17. I like **bedrooms** with Spanish or Mediterranean style **furniture**.

18. Would you please get me a **spoon** for my ice cream?

19. That **bedroom** is too small for a king-size bed.

20. My **house** is about 12 years old now; how old is your **home**?

21. At our house, the **kitchen** is a popular place.

22. Large **closets** are a very nice thing to have in a bedroom.

PRACTICE TEST 3

Lessons 7 - 8 - 9

Go through this practice test without referring back to the last three lessons to see how many of the **boldface** words you can remember the signs for. After you have gone through the test go back over the lessons to check yourself.

1. My house has three **bedrooms** but only one **bath**.

2. How would you like your eggs — **fried over** or **scrambled**?

3. We converted our **garage** into a **recreation room**.

4. My mother-in-law used to make the most delicious **oyster** dressing for **turkey**.

5. **Shrimp, crab,** and **lobster** are all favorites of mine.

6. **Traffic** was **backed up** because a car didn't **pull over** enough.

7. Our friends recently remodeled their **kitchen** and **dining room**.

8. The bride-to-be received a beautiful set of **knives, forks** and **spoons**.

9. We were **parked** near the bridge, but another car **skidded** into us.

10. **Cheese** and **crackers** make a good appetizer.

11. We are planning to paint our **laundry** and **powder room** soon.

12. My family used to raise a big **vegetable** garden; they also grew **grapes** and **strawberries**.

13. We had fresh **corn, lettuce, cabbage, tomatoes, onions, peas,** and **string beans** from the garden.

14. My wife makes a most delicious **sour cream cake**.

15. Will you please put the **glasses** and **napkins** on the table?

16. They have a beautiful **apartment** with a **foyer** and a private patio.

17. My friend wished to buy a **Cadillac**, but could only afford a **Pontiac**.

18. Please get some **milk, butter, bread, coffee, tea, sugar, eggs,** and **cookies** at the store.

19. Would you like a **hamburger, hot dog,** or **fish sandwich**?

20. We have French provincial **furniture** in the **living** and **dining rooms**.

21. I got a **parking ticket** even though I **overparked** only two or three minutes.

22. I like **apple, peach, pumpkin,** and **blueberry** pie; I also like **coconut** cream, **banana** cream, and **strawberry** pie.

LESSON 10

SIGNS FOR DIFFERENT COUNTRIES

The United States — "U.S." or "America".

Spain — Dbl. "1" at shoulders; bring out and hook one finger on other.

Sweden — "S" handshape circled at forehead; this represents "Northern countries".

Denmark — "D" circled at forehead.

Norway — "N" circled at forehead.

Finland — "F" circled at forehead.

Germany — Dbl. "5" crossed, one wrist on top of other; move fingers.

England — Grasp left hand with right.

Canada — Grasp coat or shirt lapel; shake it.

Scotland — "4" handshape; form plaid on left arm (upper arm).

Russia — Both hands on waist twice; this represents the "Cossack".

France — "F" handshape; twist up or down in semi-circle.

Italy — "I" handshape; cross on the forehead.

Holland — "Y" handshape; bring down in semi-circle in front of face.

Greece — "G" handshape; bring down the nose.

Japan — "J" handshape; slant on one eye.

China — Use index finger; slant one eye.

Africa — "A" handshape; circular motion at face — represents the idea of "Dark Continent".

India — "A" handshape; press thumb print on forehead, with thumb pointing downward, and move upward to represent the symbolic caste mark.

Vietnam — "VN".

Ireland — Use the crooked "2" handshape; move over the back of the opposite hand in a complete circle before resting on hand.

EXERCISES

Sign the following sentences, giving particular attention to the **boldface** words; fingerspell all words which cannot or should not be signed.

1. The **United States** is sometimes known as the "melting pot" of the world.

2. **Spain** is bordered on one side by mountains.

3. Many people from **Sweden** have blue eyes and fair skin.

4. **Denmark** is known for its fine stainless steel flatware.

5. During the winter in northern **Norway**, there is very little daylight.

6. **Finland** is one of four Scandanavian countries.

7. **Germany** is divided into two sections.

8. **England** is a part of the British Isles.

9. Much of **Canada** is unexplored forests.

10. **Scotland** is known for its fine wool materials.

11. **Russia** is sometimes referred to as the Soviet Union.

12. **France** is known for its many fine wines and cheese.

13. **Italy** is one of the cultural centers of the world.

14. Wind mills and tulips remind me of **Holland**.

15. **Greece** is located by the Aegean Sea.

16. Many goods sold in America come from **Japan.**

17. The principal diet of the people in **China** is rice and fish.

18. **Africa** was the cultural beginning of the black people.

19. Gallaudet has had several deaf students from **India**.

20. Belfast, **Ireland**, is now an infamous city.

LESSON 11

SIGNS FOR MAJOR U.S. CITIES

Cities

Washington — "W" handshape on shoulder; move up in 2 semi-circles.

Baltimore — "B" handshape; shake it up and down, palm facing left.

New York — "Y" handshape on left palm; slide across twice.

Boston — "B" handshape, palm facing outward; move in a slightly circular motion.

Philadelphia — "P" handshape; drop down in a sharp semi-circle.

Detroit — "D" handshape; drop down in a sharp semi-circle.

Chicago — "C" handshape; drop down in a sharp semi-circle.

Milwaukee — "G" handshape; slide across chin twice.

Columbus — "C" handshape on shoulder; movement same as for Washington.

Birmingham — "B" handshape; same movement as for Chicago.

Atlanta — "A" handshape; move from left shoulder to right.

Pittsburgh — same sign as "steel pin".

New Orleans — "O" handshape; brush down against palm, twice.

Kansas City — "K.C."

Los Angeles — "L.A."

St. Louis — Sometimes spelled out. Sometimes spelled "St. L."

Miami — Always spell out.

NOTE:
In some localities, deaf people have "local signs" for their area towns and cities, e.g.:

Richmond — "R" handshape, same movement as for Chicago.

Frederick — "F" handshape; shake the hand back and forth lightly.

EXERCISES

Sign the following sentences, giving particular attention to the **boldface** words; fingerspell all words which cannot or should not be signed.

1. Gallaudet College is located in **Washington**, D.C.

2. **Baltimore** is known for its "white" door stoops.

3. **New York** is the largest city in the United States.

4. Many important people in history have come from **Philadelphia**.

5. O'Hare Airport is located outside of **Chicago**.

6. **Detroit** is the car manufacturing center of the U.S.

7. Schlitz is the beer that made **Milwaukee** famous.

8. **Columbus** is the capital of Ohio.

9. **Birmingham** is a big steel city.

10. The Delta Airlines headquarters are in **Atlanta**, Georgia.

11. **Pittsburgh** is located in far western Pennsylvania.

12. **New Orleans** is famous for its Mardi Gras.

13. The "**Kansas City** Chiefs" is the name of a football team.

14. **Los Angeles** is in southern California.

15. The city of **St. Louis** is on the banks of the Mississippi River.

16. Many political conventions are held in **Miami**, Florida.

17. **Boston** is the capital city of Massachusetts.

18. **Richmond** is an interesting city of yesterday and today.

19. The Maryland School for the Deaf is located at **Frederick**.

LESSON 12

LOCAL COLLEGES AND UNIVERSITIES

Gallaudet College — "G" over the R eye side; bring to a close as you move back.

Catholic University — "C.U."

George Washington University — "G.W.U."

Georgetown University — "GT"

The University of Maryland — Use the "U" handshape, holding hand slightly outward; move in small circles; then spell "of Md.".

Maryland University — "Md. U."

Howard University — "Howard U."

D.C. Teachers College — "D.C. Teachers" or "D.C.T.C."

George Mason College — "G.M. College"

Southeastern University — Sign: "South" + "East" + "University".

Montgomery College — "MG College"

Federal City College — "FCC"

Prince George Community College — "P.G. College"

Washington Technical Institute — "WTI"

COMMON RELIGIONS

Catholic — "U" handshape; make cross sign on forehead.

Lutheran — "L" on back of hand; move up and down twice.

Baptist — Dbl. A handshape; Mime Sign the act of total immersion into water.

Episcopal — Index finger; move out from below wrist and down near elbow.

Seventh Day Adventist — Abbreviate "SDA".

Presbyterian — "P"; brush palm twice.

Methodist — Rub hands together.

44

Christian — Sign: "Jesus" + the "-er", meaning person.

United Brethren — "UB".

Quaker — Mesh fingers and twiddle thumbs to symbolize meditation.

Church of God — Sign literally.

Assembly of God — Spell "assembly"; sign God or Use "A" handshape in middle of forehead, move out and up to sign for "God".

Mormon (Church of Jesus Christ of Latter Day Saints) — "M" handshape on side of face; slide down over cheek two times.

Jewish (Hebrew) — Fingers over and thumb below chin; move down to symbolize a bearded patriarch.

church — "C" on back of hand; double movement.

temple — "T" on back of hand; double movement.

religion — "R" at heart; move down and out to symbolize reverent feelings.

EXERCISES

Sign the following sentences, giving particular attention to the **boldface** names; fingerspell all words which cannot or should not be signed.

1. The only liberal arts college for the deaf is **Gallaudet College**.

2. **Catholic University** is not far from Gallaudet College.

3. The **George Washington University** has a medical school of its own.

4. **Georgetown University** is located in the Northwest section of Washington, D.C.

5. The **University of Maryland** has the largest enrollment in the state of Maryland.

6. You can study Black Arts at **Howard University**.

7. **D.C. Teachers' College** is a member of the college consortium in this area.

8. **Prince George's Community College** offers credit courses in sign language.

9. **Montgomery College** in Takoma Park was formerly a junior college.

10. **Federal City College** and the **Washington Technical Institute** are the newest colleges in D.C.

11. Gallaudet plays basketball against **George Mason College** and **Southeastern University**.

12. What is your **religion**?

13. The Pope is the head of the Roman **Catholic Church**.

14. Leland Memorial Hospital in Riverdale is operated by the **Seventh Day Adventists**.

15. The Washington Cathedral is a part of the **Episcopal** Church.

16. Riverdale **Baptist Church** is one of the largest in the Washington area.

17. My mother was a **Methodist**; my father a **Lutheran**.

18. The **Mormon Temple** on 16th Street, N.W., is a beautiful structure.

19. The **Quakers** are generally known as quiet, meditating people.

20. The **Jewish** Sabbath is from sunset Friday until sunset Saturday.

PRACTICE TEST 4

Lessons 10 - 11 - 12

Go through this practice test without referring back to the last three lessons to see how many of the **boldface** words you can remember the signs for. After you have gone through the test go back over the lessons to check yourself.

1. The 1972 N.A.D. Convention was held in **Miami**, Florida.

2. Most people in the **United States** will be glad when we get out of **Vietnam**.

3. **Milwaukee** is a large city in Wisconsin.

4. **Georgetown** University is a Catholic institution.

5. **Washington, D.C.,** is a city of beautiful **churches** and **temples**.

6. Did you know that President Nixon comes from a **Quaker** family?

7. **New York, Chicago** and **Los Angeles** are America's largest cities.

8. The name "Madsen" is very common in **Denmark**.

9. On our trip, we visited **Baltimore, Philadelphia**, and **Boston.**

10. The **Seventh Day Adventist Church** operates many fine hospitals and medical centers.

11. In this area, **Baptist** churches lead in the number of interpreted services for the deaf.

12. **Howard University** and **Gallaudet College** have enjoyed athletic competition since 1950.

13. It seems that **Federal City College** and **D.C. Teachers** will not merge after all.

14. **Birmingham, Alabama,** is called the "**Pittsburgh** of the South."

15. We would love to visit **England, Ireland** and **Scotland** some day.

16. I once dreamed I was touring Moscow, **Russia**; it was an odd dream.

17. My wife spent a week in **Spain** last April.

18. She also spent two days shopping in Tangier, Morocco, in Northern **Africa**.

19. **Frederick** is the home of the Maryland School for the Deaf and Barbara Fritchie candy.

20. The **University of Maryland** has had riots the past two or three years.

21. The Hillel Club is an organization for **Jewish** students.

22. **Episcopal** students have their Canterbury Club and **Lutheran** students join the Gamma Delta.

LESSON 13

PERSON SIGNS REQUIRING ADDITION OF "-ER"

Certain words depicting persons or doers require signing only the base word plus the person or "-er" sign. For example:

believer — Sign "believe" + "-er"

actor	poet
advisor	player
buyer	preacher/pastor
dancer	seller
debater	settlers
fighter	scientist
defender	speaker
inventor	surgeon
lawyer	swimmer
leader	visitor
loser	worker
	waiter

Other words depicting persons require additional base signs. For example:

actress — Sign: "female" + "act" + "-er"

applicant — "volunteer" + "-er"

counselor — Signed like "advisor" or like "supervisor" depending on meaning desired.

critic — "criticize" + "-er"

guardian — Signed like "supervisor"

judge — "justice" + "-er"

lecturer, speaker — Use "closed - 5" handshape; palm up at 45 degree angle; shake hand up and down + "-er".

pilot/flyer — "airplane" + "-er"

pianist, typist — Mime sign act of playing a piano or typing + "-er"

receiver — (1) "get" + "-er"; (2) in football, mime sign catching a football + "-er"

student — "learn" + -"er"

supervisor — "take care of" + "-er"; "supervise"

stranger — "know" + "new" + "-er"

waitress — "female" + "wait" + "-er"

PERSON SIGNS NOT REQUIRING ADDITION OF "-ER"

doctor — "d"; nurse — "n"; psychiatrist — "p"
all signed on the pulse with 2 taps; however, "psychiatrist" requires the added "-er"

dentist — "d"   on the front teeth.

member — "m"   just below left shoulder with "m" pointed toward you; move over to just below right shoulder.

king — "k"; queen — "q"
same starting position as above with letters on body; move across body to right hip bone.

prince — "p"   position same as above with "p" pointed toward and touching you; move as in "king".

princess — "p"   position as above; move to right shoulder as in member; then down to right hip bone.

guard (meaning a "security member" or "policeman") — Mime sign "wearing a badge".

priest (Father) — Mime sign "wearing a priest's collar"

God — "B" handshape; move up above head and bring hand slightly back and down in reverent movement.

god/goddess — generally spelled out; sometimes signed as in "God" but at facial level rather than above head; goddess could be signed the same way, preceded by "female" indicator.

bachelor — "b" at right or left side of chin; move to opposite side of chin.

spinster (Old Maid) — "c" handshape; move to and from face twice over nose.

EXERCISES

Sign the following sentences, giving particular attention to the **boldface** words; fingerspell all words which cannot or should not be signed.

1. Who is your favorite **actor**?

2. Josephine wants to be an **actress**.

3. Are you an **applicant** for that job?

4. What makes a **believer**?

5. Mr. Jones is a **buyer** for the store.

6. **Counselors** should be trained.

7. Mr. Nixon has many **critics**.

8. Gallaudet has some good **dancers**.

9. Are you a good **debater**?

10. Fire**fighters** are important men.

11. **Guardians** are needed for children without parents.

12. Edison was the **inventor** of the electric light.

13. The **guard** let me in the building.

14. The **judge** refused to release the man.

15. Who is your **lawyer**?

16. We need good **leaders** for the future.

17. Good sportsmanship includes being a good **loser**.

18. The **lecturer** tonight is Mr. Madsen.

19. China and Russia appear to be political **opponents**.

20. Keats is one of my favorite **poets**.

LESSON 14

DISEASES AND ILLNESSES

mumps — Mime sign "swelling of the glands under the ears".

red measles — Mime sign "red" + "spots all over the face".

German measles — Sign "German"; then sign "measles".

chicken pox — Sign "chicken"; then spell "pox" or sign "pox" as in "measles".

pneumonia — Commonly abbreviated "pn"; may be signed, using the dbl. "B" handshape, fingertips on chest, move up and down. This sign is more commonly used for "bronchitis".

a cold — Mime sign "blowing nose" 2 or 3 times.

tuberculosis — Sign "T.B."

heart attack — Use open "8" handshape; touch area of the heart with the middle finger twice; then move hand out and quickly strike the left palm, opened in front of the heart.

heart disease — Sign "heart" as in "heart attack" but spell "disease". Sometimes the word, "disease" is signed like "illness" or "sickness".

cancer — Must be spelled out.

appendicitis — Indicated by the sign for the "operating to remove the appendix".

operation — Use "A" handshape, thumb sticking out; (the thumb will represent the surgeon's knife), move the "knife" on a part of the body to indicate where the operation takes place.

surgery — R hand in the same shape as above; L hand in a "5" handshape, palm facing right; move the "knife" on palm to indicate the "cutting open".

cerebral palsy — Use abbreviation, "C.P."

mental illness — Sign "mental"; then sign "ill".

mentally retarded — Use initials "M.R." at the right side of the temple or forehead

apply (put on) medication — Mime sign "rubbing medicine on a wound".

emergency room — Use abbreviation "E.R." but only when it is clear you are referring to a hospital.

51

hospital — Use the "H" handshape placed on opposite upper arm; form a cross shape with the "H".

infirmary — Use the "I" handshape; make the same movement with the "I" as in "hospital".

EXERCISES

Sign the following sentences, giving particular attention to the **boldface** words; fingerspell all words which cannot or should not be signed.

1. Having the **mumps** is a very uncomfortable illness.

2. A severe case of **German measles** can have the result of hearing loss.

3. One always looks funny with spots on his skin from **chicken pox**.

4. If **pneumonia** is not carefully watched, it can lead to death.

5. Drafty rooms often cause bad **colds**.

6. **Tuberculosis** is often an undetached disease.

7. **Heart disease** is usually a prolonged disease.

8. Being overweight can cause a **heart attack**.

9. Someday, hopefully, there will be a cure for **cancer**.

10. **Appendicitis** is a disease that requires immediate attention.

11. An **operation** was necessary as a result of the fall.

12. Plastic **surgery** is expensive.

13. The nurse **applied the medication** to the burned victim.

14. There are many different forms of **mental illness**.

15. **Mentally retarded** children can be helped!

16. **Cerebral palsy** is a crippling disease.

17. **Emergency rooms** must be spotlessly clean.

18. Many **hospitals** are overcrowded.

19. All schools are required to have an **infirmary**.

20. I hate to be **sick**! Don't you?

LESSON 15

GOVERNMENT AND POLITICS

government — "1" handshape near temple; curve it while moving in a circular motion letting finger come to rest on temple.

governor — <u>Sign</u>: the same as above plus "-er", meaning person.

capital — <u>Sign</u>: the same as government because a capital is the seat of government.

capitol — <u>Sign</u>: as above but add "building."

politics — "P" handshape at temple; move in a circular motion coming to rest at temple as in government.

politician — <u>Sign</u>: the same as above plus the "-er", meaning person.

political affiliation — <u>Sign</u>: "politics" plus "connection."

democratic — "D" handshape - sway back and forth.

a Republican — "R" handshape; same movement as above.

a Democrat — "D", moving as in "democratic" plus the "-er", meaning person.

president — Use the dble. "C" handshape near the forehead; move out in opposite directions and close to a dble. "S".

vice-president — Usually abbreviated "V.P."

chairman — Often signed like "captain", a "crooked 5" handshape on the R shoulder; sometimes signed literally as two words.

Congress — Use "C" handshape at L shoulder; move over to R shoulder.

legislature — Use "L" handshape; same movement as above.

committee, board — "Open C", all fingers touching the body; same movement as above. For "Board", use "B" handshape on shoulder; same movement.

senator — "S" handshape; same movement as above.

legislator — "L" handshape; same movement as above; add "-er" sign for person.

representative — Abbreviated "rep."

law/legal — "L" handshape flat against opposite palm; move out and down against palm once.

legislation, legislative — Use "L" handshape; same movement as for "law" except that the thumb touches L palm.

EXERCISES

Sign the following sentences, giving particular attention to the **boldface** words; fingerspell all words which cannot or should not be signed.

1. **Congress** is made up of the House of **Representatives** and the **Senate**.

2. The **legislature** will decide on the bill Monday.

3. **Committee A** of the Undergraduate Faculty meets frequently in Hall Memorial Building.

4. The **Board** of Directors of the college meets here regularly.

5. **Senator** Magnuson spoke at the Gallaudet Commencement last May.

6. A **congressman** is a **legislator**.

7. The state **legislature** is behind in its work this year.

8. The **Democratic National Convention** was held this year in Miami.

9. A study of **politics** should be interesting.

10. The **Governor** of Alabama was shot at a **political** rally in Maryland.

11. The White House is the home of all our **Presidents**.

12. Do you know the names of your **Congressman** and your **Senator**?

13. The Louisiana state **capitol** is a beautiful, tall building.

14. There is an old saying something like this: "**Politicians** make strange bed-fellows."

15. **Legislation** affecting the deaf is always important to us.

16. Are you a **Republican** or a **Democrat**?

17. One gets a **legal** opinion from his lawyer.

18. Baton Rouge is the **capital** city of Louisiana. The name means "red stick."

19. The **government** of the United States is a huge organization.

20. Who is the new **Chairman** of the Armed Forces **Committee**?

PRACTICE TEST 5

Lessons 13 - 14 - 15

Go through this practice test without referring back to the last three lessons to see how many of the **boldface** words you can remember the signs for. After you have gone through the test go back over the lessons to check yourself.

1. Have you witnessed a joint session of **Congress**?

2. Do you know a good **psychiatrist** in this area?

3. Joe was in the **hospital** six days after his hernia **operation**.

4. My wife is sometimes my best **critic** and **judge**.

5. I worked briefly for **Senator** John F. Kennedy before he became **President**.

6. The **bachelor** and the **spinster** met and married after a quick courtship.

7. Rubella or the **German measles** is a dreaded disease for pregnant women.

8. **Politics** and **politicians** make an interesting topic for discussion.

9. My youngest brother is a **professor** of piano.

10. Have you ever had the **mumps** or the **chicken pox**?

11. Who is the new **Chairman** of the **Board** of Directors?

12. Every state sends two **Senators** to Washington, but the number of **Representatives** depends on population.

13. The **lecture** was presented by a very charming **speaker**.

14. It is hard to find a good **doctor** and a good **dentist** in a large city.

15. I had to take my little boy to the **hospital emergency room**.

16. Where will the **Republicans** hold their national convention this year?

17. The **capital** of Kansas is Topeka which is an Indian name.

18. The national **capitol** has an interesting history.

19. **Vice-President** Agnew was formerly **Governor** of Maryland.

20. What is the **legal** speed limit in Wyoming?

21. **Pneumonia** caused my wife's deafness when she was five.

22. The stranger suffered a **heart attack** on the sidewalk.

LESSON 16

USE OF COMPARATIVES AND SUPERLATIVES

In signing comparatives and superlatives, first sign the base word and then make the "-er" with a short "most" motion; the "-est" with a higher "most" motion. If the comparative or superlative is preceded by "more" or "most", sign these words separately from the base word.

Positive	Comparatives	Superlatives
nice	nicer	nicest
clean	cleaner	cleanest
close (near)	closer (nearer)	closest (nearest)
good	better	best
long	longer	longest
pretty	prettier	prettiest
smart	smarter	smartest
beautiful	more beautiful	most beautiful
famous	more famous	most famous

EXERCISES

Sign the following sentences, giving particular attention to the **boldface** words; fingerspell all words which cannot or should not be signed.

1. This room is **cleaner** than that room.

2. Where is the **closest** gas station?

3. Can you tell me the **best** way to get there?

4. John thinks he is **smarter** than Jim.

5. Today seemed like the **longest** day.

6. Who is **more famous**, Washington or Lincoln?

7. Sometimes men are the **weaker** sex.

8. Your dress is **shorter** than mine.

9. I think Linda is the **prettiest** girl.

10. **Better** communication is our goal.

LESSON 17

SOME VERB PROBLEMS

"DO"

When do you sign "DO"? Spell "do" when used as a question or in an expression like:

"How do you do?" — Spell the "dos".

"Do you do that all the time?" — Spell 1st "do"; sign 2nd "do".

"Do you know who does that job?" — Spell "do"; sign "does".

"Does the President do much work?" — Spell "does"; sign "do".

"HAVE"

have — (1) (possessive) Use the sign, "have". (2) (as an auxiliary verb) Use the sign "finish".

have to — Sign: "must", spell: "to", as in: "I have to leave now."

"USED TO"

Don't confuse with "used to" as an adverb of time. Sign like "habit" or "accustomed to".

EXAMPLE: (note the difference)

"I used to wrestle." — Sign "long ago".

"I am used to going to town every day." — Sign: "habit" + "to".

"X" HANDSHAPE SIGNS OF SIMILARITY

must — Use one strong movement down

have to — Sign "must" + "to"

need, necessary, necessity — Use repeated up-down movements.

supposed to — Sign: "should" + "to"

suppose (as a verb) — Sign: "imagine" except for short, rapidly-repeated movement.

LOOK, SEE, OBSERVE

see — Use the "2" handshape to represent the eyes; move forward from the eyes in the line of vision.

watch, look — <u>Sign</u>: "see" but with two fingers pointing directly outward from the eyes to the object. Dbl. handshape may be used for emphasis.

observe — <u>Sign</u>: "watch" with dbl. "2" handshape, fingers pointing toward object to be observed.

THE VERB "TO BE"

Accepted today are the new signed English forms of the verb "to be".

be — <u>Sign</u> like "true" with "B" handshape.

am — <u>Sign</u> as above with "A" handshape.

is — <u>Sign</u> as above with "I" handshape.

are — <u>Sign</u> as above with "R" handshape.

was — Use "W" handshape at mouth; move back around side of face and change to an "S" handshape.

were — <u>Sign</u> same as above but change to an "R" handshape.

EXERCISES

Sign the following sentences, giving particular attention to the **boldface** words; fingerspell all words which cannot or should not be signed.

1. **See** your teacher after class.

2. **Watch** carefully how I do it.

3. **Do** we **have** any more coffee?

4. **Have** you ever **observed** a squirrel hoarding nuts?

5. **Look!** The sun is shining again!

6. I **have to** sit down and finish this letter.

7. One never gets **used to** living in a hot, humid city.

8. I've become **used to** signing all the time.

9. Getting enough sleep is a **must** for me.

10. It became a **necessity** to take her to the store.

11. The side comments of the viewers were not **necessary**.

12. The family was **supposed to** meet me here at 12:30.

13. Let's **suppose** that you had $500.00. What would you do?

14. It can't **be** the truth!

15. All the birds **are** happy because their birdbath is full of water.

16. I **am** very pleased with your progress.

17. They **were** not prepared for the shock.

18. She **was** not happy with her test scores.

19. **Watch** Jim dive into the pool.

20. Please **observe** how Judy **watches** the birds.

LESSON 18

SOME ACTION WORDS AND PHRASES

"Please pay attention!"

wash the dishes — R hand palm rubs the L hand palm in circular movements.

wash clothes — Use dbl. "A" handshapes; same circular movement, or simply rub back and forth.

wash the car — Mime Sign: washing over a car top or hood, using the dble. "A" handshape.

wash your face — Mime Sign: washing your face with palms of hands.

wash your hands — Mime Sign: washing the hands.

wash the walls — Mime Sign: "washing the walls", using the dbl. "A" handshape and moving hands.

drive a car — Mime Sign: steering a car.

drive a horse — Mime Sign: driving horses with reins.

look at someone — Sign: "see" with the "2" handshape pointing outward toward person or object looked at or watched.

watch . . . me — Sign as above, but turn fingers toward yourself.

look for — Sign: "hunt" + "for".

60

pay attention — Use dbl. "5" handshape, one hand near each side of the face and move outward towards the object of attention.

concentrate — <u>Sign</u>: "pay attention" with more emphasis.

pay attention to me — Reverse movement of "pay attention" so that hands are out in front of your face and move back toward the sides of your face.

be careful — <u>Sign</u>: "careful"

watch out — <u>Sign</u>: "careful" with only one movement; spell "out".

EXERCISES

Sign the following sentences, giving particular attention to the **boldface** words and phrases; fingerspell all words which cannot or should not be signed.

1. **Watch** Jim dive into the pool.

2. Sometimes it is hard to **pay attention**.

3. Can you **concentrate** with all that noise?

4. Please **look at me** while I explain this sign.

5. Always **pay** close **attention** to your work.

6. Betty must **wash the dishes** tonight.

7. How often do you **wash your car**?

8. Little Bobby did not **wash his face**.

9. **Washing** painted **walls** is rather hard work.

10. Did you try **washing your hands** with lava soap?

11. **Driving** used to be a real pleasure.

12. My mother used to **wash the clothes** by hand, using a scrub board.

13. As a boy, I enjoyed **driving** a team of horses pulling a hay wagon.

14. Did you **look for** your lost watch?

15. You should **be careful** how you **wash** nylons.

16. When you cross the street, always **watch out** for cars.

17. Bob said to **watch out** for Mary; she is in a bad mood.

18. Did you ever **watch** a drunk trying to **drive** straight?

19. Don't use hard detergents when you **wash your car**.

20. My wife wants a new dishwasher; she is tired of **washing dishes**.

21. Our old **dishwasher** is broken and cannot be fixed.

22. The Amish in Pennsylvania still **drive horses** and carriages.

PRACTICE TEST 6

Lessons 16 - 17 - 18

Go through this practice test without referring back to the last three lessons to see how many of the **boldface** words you can remember the signs for. After you have gone through the test go back over the lessons to check yourself.

1. **Watch** your driving, don't **look at** me!

2. Jim is very smart, but I think Bob is **smarter**.

3. **Do** you **have** an extra copy or **do** you **have to** make one?

4. The **best** restaurants in Washington are not necessarily the **most expensive**.

5. My mother **used to drive a horse** and buggy.

6. My mother never learned to **drive a car**.

7. You must **pay attention to** your instructor.

8. After you **wash the dishes**, you may start **washing the clothes**.

9. Which President do you think was the **most famous**?

10. We **have to do** our work or we will lose our jobs.

11. Please **wash your hands** before you go out to play.

12. That dress is pretty, but I think this dress is **prettier**.

13. Is it **necessary** to **watch** the soup closely?

14. Would you help Daddy **wash the car** this afternoon?

15. I was **supposed to** go to Baltimore but my plans were cancelled.

16. Do you **suppose** it is all right if I **observe** your class?

17. It is hard to get **used to** hot, muggy weather.

18. Jean is about two inches **taller** than Shirley.

19. Would you like to **observe** Mr. Berke's class tonight?

20. We **need** to **have** the roof fixed before long.

21. Spring cleaning is such a chore when you **have to wash the walls**.

22. Where is the **closest** gas station?

LESSON 19

PREFIXES AND SUFFIXES

In recent years, a number of sign formations for prefixes and suffixes have grown out of programs endeavoring to imitate English morphemes to give the deaf child more precise English. Some such signs have existed for a long time such as the negative prefixes, for example; others are relatively new, an outgrowth of the S.E.E. program. We offer some of the more commonly known ones here for general information and knowledge. They may be useful in many circumstances, but it should be understood that they are not a part of the sign language the average deaf person presently uses.

PREFIXES

pre- — Sign: "before" using the "P" handshape.

post- — Sign: "after" using the "P" handshape.

PREFIXES MEANING "NOT"

dis-; un-; il-; in-; im- — Use the formal negative sign for the prefix followed by the base word. The formal negative is made by crossing hands at wrists and moving out in opposite directions; however, it is best to spell the prefix first and then sign the negative meaning plus the base word. [For example: "unhappy" — you would spell "un", sign "happy" and then repeat in signs: "not" + "happy".]

SUFFIXES

-ing — Use the "I" handshape, move sraight from L to R once.

-d, -ed, -t — Past forms are generally indicated by spelled endings in manual English.

-s, -es — Plural endings likewise are added by spelling.

-ish — Use the "I" handshape in a downward zig-zag movement.

-ion, -tion — Use the "I" handshape with the R thumb against L fingers; let the R hand slide down L palm.

-ment — Bring the "M" handshape on R hand to a rest at center of open L palm with index finger touching palm.

-ness — Position the "N" handshape as above but let is slide down L palm.

-ful — Generally spelled out.

-ly — Always spelled out.

EXERCISES

Sign the following sentences, giving particular attention to the **boldface** affixes; fingerspell all words which cannot or should not be signed.

1. Twin sisters and brothers are often **in**separable.

2. We sometimes have an **in**adequate supply of water.

3. The **pre**-tourney activities were dull.

4. Jerry must go to the doctor for a **post**-operative visit.

5. Are you **dis**satisfied with my work?

6. We will be work**ing** late tonight.

7. I want**ed** to go, but I didn't have enough money.

8. The **im**mature young lady acted very brash.

9. That answer seems **il**logical.

10. Girl**ish** hairdos are cute on some young women.

11. The advance**ment** of all the deaf is what we need.

12. Mary's cheerful**ness** kept everyone happy.

13. The boys desir**ed** to win bad**ly**.

14. The suc**tion** pump does not work today.

15. You were all very help**ful**, thank you.

16. Recent develop**ments** kept everyone very busy.

17. Happi**ness** is a double dip ice cream cone!

18. Her wish**es** were that no one be made **im**patient.

19. Starting tomorrow we will keep add**ing** new words.

20. That little girl has a pair of the most devil**ish**-looking eyes.

LESSON 20

MIXED WORD GROUPS

In signing the following terms, first sign the possessive pronoun with palm outward toward whoever or whatever is indicated; repeat movement immediately adding emphasis for "own".

his own   your own
her own   their own
its own

For "my own", sign "mine".
For "our own", sign "ours" with a little force.

For phrases like: "I own_____", you may either spell the word, "own" or sign it like the possessive "have".

To sign the apostrophe form showing possessiveness in names (Betty's) spell out the person's name and then with the "S" handshape, twist your hand and wrist sharply to the right.

FUN vs. FUNNY

Do not confuse these two ideas. They are different in signs as well as meaning.

funny — "N" handshape; brush down on nose a couple of times.

fun — Dbl. "N" handshape; brush R "N" down on nose once and then strike L "N" down and back up.

BORROW vs. LOAN (LEND)

Dbl. "2" handshape, one hand resting on other; movement is either in or out in semi-circle, in for "borrow" and out for "loan" or "lend".

"loan me"/"lend me" — Same as "borrow" except movement comes almost straight in.

If you want to say: "He borrowed my book", simply change the direction of "borrow" toward "him".

POSITIVE - NEGATIVE

Use the dbl. "1" handshape; position as a "plus" for positive.

Use the "1" handshape positioned as a "minus" against the L palm for negative.

66

PROGRAM vs. PROJECT

program — Use the "P" handshape on R hand; position inside L hand palm facing right, below little finger; slide down; then move to back of hand below little finger and slide down.

project — Same position and movement as "program" but change "P" to "J" when moving to back of L hand.

PERFECT/EXACT/PRECISE

perfect — Use the dbl. "P" handshape, L palm facing you and R palm facing the L; bring the "P's" together, middle fingers touching, after a slight circular movement.

exact — Same position and movement as above but with the dbl. "F" handshape or closed "F" handshape.

precise — Same position as above but with dbl. "P" handshape; move "P's" precisely together without any circular movement.

EXERCISES

Sign the following sentences, giving particular attention to the **boldface** words; fingerspell all words which cannot or should not be signed.

1. Bob and Bill brought **their own** lunches.

2. Do you **own** a bicycle?

3. Water skiing is great **fun** for some people.

4. The clown looked so **funny** when he fell.

5. Would you please **lend** me a quarter?

6. I don't like to **borrow** money.

7. What is the **precise** diet plan for weight watchers?

8. The **loan** was approved by the bank.

9. Did you see **Jerry's** boat?

10. Try to be **positive**, not **negative**, O.K.?

11. The **project** will continue throughout the year.

12. I **lent** my book to John yesterday.

13. **Mary's** boy friend called five times last night.

14. Jeanne wanted the puppy for **her own**.

15. Why don't you buy **your own** car?

16. That table is **ours**, not **yours**.

17. We had a lot of **fun** at the party.

18. Wouldn't it be **funny** if we saw a Martian?

19. I need to **borrow** two dollars.

20. Do you know where **Jerry's** house is?

LESSON 21

MIXED WORD GROUPS

character (meaning one's inner self) — Use "C" handshape at L shoulder; move in complete circle, coming to rest at shoulder area above heart.

character (meaning one in a play or story) — Use "C" handshape at L palm facing right; move as above, coming to rest on L palm. [This indicates a portrayal or showing of a character.]

personality (meaning the sum of what one is) — Use "P" handshape in the same movement for one's character at L shoulder area.

personality (meaning a person) — Sign: "person".

attitude — Use "A" handshape in the same movement as one's character and personality, at L shoulder area.

grandchildren — Use "G" handshape near R forehead or temple; move out in two semi-circular movements to indicate "future" and then Sign: "children". [This is opposite of "grandfather" which is "father" plus a movement towards the past.]

grandson — Same handshape and movement as above + Sign: "son".

granddaughter — Same as above + Sign: "daughter".

great-grandchildren — Use the same handshape as above, but increase movement to three (3) semi-circular movements.

weigh/weight, pounds, scales — Use the dbl. "H" handshape with palms facing each other; place one "H" on top of the other and move top one the same as a scale balancing.

duty — Use the "D" handshape on R hand; place on back of L hand, palm down; lift "D" and drop down again.

function — Same movement as above but with "F" handshape.

train (railroad/choo choo) — Use the dbl. "H" handshape, palms facing downward; cross the R "H" on top of the L "H" and move back and forth.

train (new teachers) — Sign: "practice" using the "T" handshape.

area — Sign: "place" using the dbl. "A" handshape.

position — Sign: "place" but with middle fingers of the dbl. "P" handshape touching each other.

69

situation (meaning "place" or "position") — <u>Sign</u>: "place" using the dbl. "S" handshape.

environment — Use the "E" handshape on R hand and the "1" handshape on L; move "E" halfway around the "1".

circumstances — <u>Sign</u>: "environment" using the "C" handshape.

situation (meaning circumstance) — <u>Sign</u>: "environment" using the "S" handshape.

chance — <u>Sign</u>: "allow".

permit — <u>Sign</u>: "allow" but with dbl. "P" handshape.

opportunity — <u>Sign</u>: like "allow" but with initial 'O" handshape, moving forward to a "P" handshape.

assist, assistance — <u>Sign</u> like "help" but use the dbl. "A" handshape and push L hand up with R "A".

support — <u>Sign</u> as above but with dbl. "S" handshape.

reinforce — <u>Sign</u>: "support" but use "R" handshape on R hand or use dbl. "R" handshape, L "R" on top of R "R"; push L "R" up with R.

EXERCISES

Sign the following sentences, giving particular attention to the **boldface** words; fingerspell all words which cannot or should not be signed.

1. Mrs. Jones who has an interesting **personality** is an interesting **personality**.

2. We have one **grandson**; do you have any **grandchildren**?

3. I have a **weight** problem since I quit smoking.

4. Your **scales** are not accurate!

5. What is the **function** of the Vice-President's office?

6. Do your **duty**; protect your **environment**.

7. **Circumstances** put Bill in an awkward **position**.

8. Would you like to **assist** with this **project**?

9. The **situation** here was bad enough after Hurricane Agnes.

10. The teachers in **training** went to New York by **train**.

11. Total communication gives us an **opportunity** to **reinforce** learning.

12. My home is **situated** on a hill in Riverdale overlooking Washington.

13. What did your **granddaughter weigh** at birth?

14. Larry's **attitude** has improved very much.

15. Who was that TV **character** with a bad **character**?

16. This **area** needs more **environmental** controls.

17. Whom will you **support** in the meeting?

18. We have a **duty** to **train** many more interpreters for the deaf in the U.S.

19. I need **assistance** with this **training program**.

20. I **weighed** only six pounds at birth, but look at me now!

PRACTICE TEST 7

Lessons 19 - 20 - 21

Go through this practice test without referring back to the last three lessons to see how many of the **boldface** words you can remember the signs for. After you have gone through the test go back over the lessons to check yourself.

1. That course requires a **pre**-test and a **post**-test.

2. Jeanne has a boy**ish** personality, but she is cute!

3. Bill and Bob had a disagree**ment** over which **project** was more important.

4. The Sign Language **Programs** office handles several different **programs**.

5. A **positive attitude** is better than a **negative attitude**.

6. It would be **funny** if we found the **scales imperfect**.

7. What kind of **environment** would you like to retire to?

8. The verb "to be" has several **functions**; to link, to show state of being or to help another verb.

9. Your kind**ness** in this **situation** is appreciat**ed**.

10. Sometimes kids have a devil**ish attitude**.

11. We will need your **exact** measurements.

12. **Opportunities** for **reinforcement** in learning are very important.

13. It is **im**possible to have a **perfect environment**.

14. My parents have 24 **grandchildren** and 13 **great-grandchildren**.

15. May we borrow your **book** on **fun**-times?

16. Mary said it was **her own** idea to **assist** us.

17. Please **lend** me your **support**, will you?

18. What is the Washington **area** famous for?

19. Agnew and Eagleton make two interesting **character** studies.

20. Who is your favorite comic strip **character**?

21. The **function** of government should be to **assist** people in need.

22. Let's study the **character** of Benjamin Franklin.

LESSON 22

MIXED WORD GROUPS

then — "next" - "L" handshape position on the L hand, palm facing the body and index finger pointing to the R. With the index position on the R hand, palm facing to the left, start at the back of the thumb ending with the tip of the R index finger ending on the L index finger.

than — used with comparatives. Dbl. "B" handshape; L palm down; R palm facing L hand; move R hand so fingers strike past L hand fingers.

obey — flat "O" handshape position on both hands with tips touching forehead and move hands down.

inform, notify, let (me) (you) know — Flat "O" handshape position on both hands with tips touching forehead and move hands out.

depend, dependence — "hang" sign with R index finger over L index finger, but move fingers up and down a couple of times.

dependent — (person). Sign as above) add "-er".

feel, emotion — Use open "8" handshape, one hand; two movements.

excite, thrill — Same handshape, but bring fingers up only once, rather rapidly.

exciting, thrilling — Same handshape, but alternate movement of both hands a few times.

inspire, inspiration — Use whole hand(s); open "5" handshape below chest; move upward once.

sick — (1) In extreme disgust, sign "turns my stomach". (2) Literally, dbl. open "8" handshape on forehead and stomach.

sick of — In feeling, single open "8" handshape on forehead; move hand in arch with finger remaining on forehead.

moon — moon/light

sun — sun/light or sun/shine

73

EXERCISES

Sign the following sentences, giving particular attention to the **boldface** words; fingerspell all words which cannot or should not be signed.

1. They will arrive at 6:00; **then** we will go.

2. This picture is better **than** that one.

3. Please **obey** your mother.

4. Please **inform** Mary about the meeting.

5. Bill and John have been **notified.**

6. **Let me know** if you can go.

7. I will **let you know** by tomorrow.

8. I am **depending** on you to help.

9. How many **dependents** do you have?

10. Do you **feel** all right?

11. That child seems **emotionally** disturbed.

12. Monkeys **excite** the children.

13. What an **exciting** game that was!

14. John was **thrilled** with the prize.

15. Mary was **inspired** to sing.

16. Writing poetry requires **inspiration.**

17. I was **sick** with a bad cold.

18. I am **sick of** this weather.

19. The **moon** is full tonight.

20. **Moonlight** sometimes affects lovers.

21. The sun is **shining** again.

22. An eclipse of the **sun** is interesting.

MIXED WORD GROUPS

"I suspect you!"

suspect, suspicious, detect — Use "1" handshape; scratch forehead a couple of times, moving out each time to an "X".

include, inclusive — Use "5" handshape on R hand; "Open-C" on L palm facing right; move "5" as in "gathering together" and place closed "5" in the "Open-C".

altogether — Signed as above (include).

all together — Signed like "cooperate" preceded by "all".

already — Signed like "finish", using dbl. "5" handshape.

all ready — (1) Move "Rs" from L to R simultaneously, usually in the sense of being ready for a trip, a speech, etc.

(2) Cross wrists; then move "Rs" out in opposite direction in the sense of being ready for a game, a race, etc.

running around — Use dbl. "1" handshape, one finger pointing up and the other down; move around rapidly in circles.

busy, business — Use dbl. "B" handshape, wrists touching each other; slide R hand "B" back and forth.

savings account — <u>Sign</u> 1st word "put money in a bank box"; spell out 2nd word.

appointment — Use "S" handshape on L hand kept still; "A" handshape on R hand, move in a circular motion and place on top of L hand.

engagement — (1) same as "appointment", but use "E" handshape instead.
(2) "being engaged to marry", use "E" handshape; same movement as "appointment" or "reservation" but over the third finger, left hand, coming to rest on that finger.

reservation — Use same as "appointment", but use "R" handshape.

aim, goal, objective — Dbl. index finger handshape; hold left hand up; move R hand toward left moderately. Use initial dbl. letter handshape for <u>goal</u> and <u>ob</u>-jective.

EXERCISES

Sign the following sentences, giving particular attention to the **boldface** words; fingerspell all words which cannot or should not be signed.

1. Mary **suspects** that Bill is not well.

2. John was very **suspicious** about the broken window.

3. The odor can be **detected** by a sensitive nose.

4. The room rate **includes** meals.

5. The tax is **included** with the room rate.

6. **Altogether** there are over 1,000 students here.

7. We will all work **together**.

8. She left **already**.

9. Are you **all ready** to go?

10. The team captain asked, "Are you **all ready**?"

11. She has been **running around** all morning.

12. Mary is very **busy** right now.

13. **Business** has been good lately.

14. Jane opened her **savings account** yesterday.

15. Jack has an **appointment** with his boss this afternoon.

16. Did you hear of Lori's **engagement**?

17. Do you have a **reservation** here?

18. My **aim** is to finish college.

19. What is your future **goal**?

20. **Objectives** should be listed for each course.

LESSON 24

MIXED WORD GROUPS

former — Sign like "past".

court, courtroom, courthouse — Sign like "judge"; dbl. "F" handshape, alternately moving up and down in front of you; "room" and "house" may be added to the latter two.

look for, search, seek, hunt — These are all signed similarly. If you mean "hunt" in the sense of going hunting, mime sign aiming with a gun, moving up and down slightly.

meaning, purpose, intention, intent, intend — These are signed similarly except that for "purpose" and "intent" you begin with the "think" sign, followed by the sign for "mean".

cause ("make happen") — Use dbl. "A" handshape, palms facing upward, move hands out and down, opening to a dbl. "5".

cause ("goal" or "purpose") — Sign like "aim" or "goal".

tend to tendency — Use open "8" handshape with one finger on chest below the heart; move up like for feel, then move out.

persuade, persuasion — Signed like "urge" in the sense of trying to make someone do something.

effort, attempt — May be signed like "try" with initial letter.

ability, expertness, expert — Signed like "skill".

announce, announcement, statement, declaration, declare — These are signed about the same; dbl. "1" handshape at mouth; move out in opposing directions

possible, possibility — May be signed "can-can" rather fast.

EXERCISES

Sign the following sentences, giving particular attention to the **boldface** words; fingerspell all words which cannot or should not be signed.

1. Sue was a **former** model.

2. In Pennsylvania, marriage licenses must be obtained at a **courthouse**.

3. Bill must go to **court** tomorrow.

4. Many people today are **searching** for their goal in life.

5. "Hide and go **seek**" is an old game.

6. **Hunting** just to kill is cruel and ruthless.

7. What is your **purpose** for this meeting?

8. In the end, his good **intentions** were not successful.

9. What was **intended** in this meaning?

10. Slippery roads **cause** accidents.

11. My **cause** in life is to be happily successful as an individual.

12. He has a **tendency** to catch colds easily.

13. Try to **persuade** him to our way of thinking.

14. It is always better to make an **effort** than to simply give up.

15. Do not **attempt** to catch me!

16. Do you have the **ability** to be an interpreter?

17. He is an **expert** skiier.

18. Their wedding **announcement** was handwritten.

19. Will peace ever be **declared** in Vietnam?

20. There is a **possibility** that the river will overflow.

PRACTICE TEST 8

Lessons 22 - 23 - 24

Go through this practice test without referring back to the last three lessons to see how many of the **boldface** words you can remember the signs for. After you have gone through the test go back over the lessons to check yourself.

1. It is a good idea to **inform** someone when you are not going to be on time due to **sickness**.

2. The children were so **excited** by the fireworks.

3. During a lunar eclipse the **sun** is behind the **moon**.

4. Being independent is better **than** being **dependent**.

5. The music was filled with **emotion** that **thrilled** us.

6. John became **suspicious** when he saw the man leave quickly.

7. Try to **include** everyone in the ball game.

8. If we **all** work **together** and **obey** the rules, we can win.

9. Jack has **already** gone home for the day; you will have to make an **appointment** for tomorrow.

10. The **business** office is usually very hectic.

11. A **savings account** is a type of insurance for the future.

12. Please make plane **reservations** for tomorrow, if **possible**.

13. Judy's **engagement** party was fun.

14. Sometimes it is easier to save money if you have a **goal**.

15. My former boss was very **busy**, and he did a lot of **running around**.

16. **Look for** the **courthouse** in the center of town.

17. The FBI **searched** for the dangerous man for weeks.

18. Wine has a **tendency** of putting me to sleep.

19. He is an **expert** glass cutter.

20. He **declared** his **feelings** for her on the night of their **engagement**.

21. I'm not sure John understood the **intentions** of the older man.

22. If we don't play cards **then** we will go to the movies.

LESSON 25

MIXED WORD GROUPS

off and on, so-so — Use one hand - palm facing left - move hand back and forth; slow, larger movement for "off and on"; a little faster for "so-so".

elevator — Use "E" handshape on R hand - move "E" up index finger of the L hand.

funeral — Use "V" handshape on both hands, one "V" ahead of the other; move both forward slowly to indicate a slow, watching march.

rebel, disobey, strike (go on strike) — These are signed similarly - except that the emphasis may be stronger on "rebel" and "strike"; use "S" handshape, holding fist up - make a sharp, short twist of the wrist and hand to the right.

simultaneously, at the same time — (1) Use the dbl. "L" handshape, palms facing downward; cross the index fingers at the tip and move both down and out in one rapid stroke. Follow by signing "time". This indicates two things happening at the same time. (2) Another way is to sign "time" followed immediately by the dbl. "Y" sign meaning "same".

influence, effect (n), affect (v) — Signed similarly - use flat "O" handshape on top of the back of left hand - move out forward, slowly spreading fingers out to an open "5" handshape. Same sign except for initial "E" for "effect".

advice (n) — Sign the same as "influence" except repeat movement more rapidly.

apply — (1) "use". (2) "volunteer for". (3) "file for". (4) "fit" or "agree with" in taste, making the sign a short distance from the face rather than at the chin.

application — Sign according to meaning: use, thing, or act. When speaking of an application form, sign "volunteer" + "paper" or mime sign a sheet of paper.

applicant — A person who applies for a job or position; make the "person" sign after signing "volunteer".

EXERCISES

Sign the following sentences, giving particular attention to the **boldface** words; fingerspell all words which cannot or should not be signed.

1. It rains **on and off** during the summer.

2. I think the weather is **so-so**.

3. The **elevator** is broken.

4. **Funerals** are sad occasions.

5. The boy **rebelled** against his mother.

6. Rules should not be **disobeyed**.

7. The workers voted to **strike**.

8. Mary was laughing and crying **simultaneously**.

9. Don't let Bill **influence** you.

10. The **effects** of TLC (tender loving care) are wonderful!

11. Weather **affects** us in many ways.

12. My **advice** to you is: "Be careful!"

13. My doctor **advised** me to stop smoking.

14. **Apply** what you have learned. [sign: "use"]

15. Will you **apply** for that job (position). [sign: "volunteer for"]

16. I have **applied** for that position. [sign: "file for" in the sense of filing an application]

17. That rule does not **apply** here. [sign: "agree" in sense of fitting]

18. Where is my **application**?

19. Do you know the **applicant**?

20. Can you spell "cat" on one hand and "dog" on the other at the **same time**?

MIXED WORD GROUPS

"Come right away!"

get (receive) — Sign as in "receive".

get (become) — Sign as in "become".

conceive — "think up" or "make up" (invent).

conceive (meaning "give life to"), impregnate — Dbl. "4" handshape; bring "4" together intertwined.

right now, right away — Sign as one word with emphasis on now.

right away — May be signed like "immediately"; "quickly".

evade, evasion, evader (person), avoid, avoidance, back out from, keep away from — These ideas have basically the same movement in signs: dbl. "A" handshape, right hand behind the left; move R hand back crookedly.

plenty — Use "S" handshape on L hand, palm facing right and open "5" handshape on R hand; place the "5" on the L hand and move out in one strong movement.

enough, sufficient — Same as in "plenty" except to move out in repeated movements.

full — The opposite movement of "plenty".

overflow — Move the "5" handshape over the "S" as in "plenty" but with the fingers wiggling or "flowing" the movement would mean "overflow" or "running over" in the sense of overflowing.

overlook — Use the "5" handshape, palm facing in or toward your face; move hand past face (eyes) in a short semi-circle.

charge (fine) — Signed like "price" or cost; "X" handshape on R hand "5" on the L, palm facing right; strike "X" down on L palm.

charge (account) — Sign like "filing" an application except you repeat movement 2 or 3 times.

charge (rush at) — The handshape will depend on who is doing the "charging" a person, an army, or an animal. Mime sign the action.

needy — Same as "difficult" except for repeated movements. [Sign more slowly].

EXERCISES

Sign the following sentences, giving particular attention to the **boldface** words; fingerspell all words which cannot or should not be signed.

1. Diane **got** her degree from Elizabethtown College.

2. Would you please **get** my purse for me?

3. How could anyone **conceive** such a crazy idea?

4. Sue's first baby was **conceived** during her honeymoon.

5. Go to it **right away**!

6. **Right now** I don't have the car.

7. One should not **evade** responsibility.

8. Lois **keeps away from** roses.

9. There is **plenty** of food in the refrigerator.

10. That's **enough**!!

11. There is not **sufficient** evidence against him.

12. The gas tank is **full**.

13. Jack **overlooks** her faults.

14. The saleslady over-**charged** me for the dress.

15. Every adult should have a **charge account** of his own.

16. The bull **charged** at the red flag.

17. There are **needy** children all over the world.

18. Mr. Smith was an income tax **evader**.

19. For contempt of court, one can be **charged** a fee or be thrown out of court.

20. I am going to **get** mad if you don't stop.

LESSON 27

MIXED WORD GROUPS

selfish — Dbl. "2" handshape, palms facing down; bring both hands back, crooking the "2"s.

miserly — Can be signed the same way as "selfish" but with more emphasis. Another way to sign is by "scratching" the L palm, indicating the "taking and keeping all you can get."

guilt, guilty, conscience — These are signed the same way. Use "G" handshape, tapping chest over heart several times; "1" for "conscience".

apprehension — This may be signed as above or signed as "fear".

conscious (mental) — Same handshape and movement as "conscience" except that you tap the R temple.

being conscious, consciousness — If you want to say: "He has regained consciousness.", you would simply sign: "He is awake again."

being aware of something, awareness — Sign "know" twice.

unconscious — Mime sign by closing eyes and letting hands drop down.

a notice (n) — Mime sign indicating a piece of paper posted.

notice (v) — Use "1" handshape on R hand; L hand out in "5", palm facing in; bring the "1" from the eye to the palm.

satisfy, relief — Signed similarly with appropriate expression; dbl. "B" handshape on chest, one hand below other; move both down.

embarrass — Dbl. "5" handshape, palms facing your face; move hands up and down in small circles in front of face. (Sometimes made with a strong, swift upward movement, to indicate extreme embarrassment.)

strict, harsh — Crooked "2" handshape in front of face; bring back sharply to nose. Sometimes "harsh" is signed like "tough".

EXERCISES

Sign the following sentences, giving particular attention to the **boldface** words; fingerspell all words which cannot or should not be signed.

1. John is a **selfish** person.

2. Scrooge was **miserly** all the time.

3. She has a **guilt** complex.

4. Martin felt **guilty** about the accident.

5. Don't you have any **conscience**?

6. A two-year old child shows his **apprehension** when approached by strangers.

7. Bobby was **being conscious** about the whole thing.

8. Joan was **conscious** during the childbirth.

9. He has regained **consciousness**.

10. Janet is **aware of** her bad qualities.

11. The parents were not **aware of** their baby's hearing loss.

12. Bill was **unconscious** after the accident.

13. There is a **notice** for the SBG from their President.

14. John **noticed** that the hub caps were missing from his car.

15. A good meal is very **satisfying**.

16. That is a **relief** to know that they are safe.

17. When I am **embarrassed**, I turn red!

18. The Dean of that school is very **strict**.

19. His tone of voice was very **harsh**.

20. The **notice** arrived today in the mail.

PRACTICE TEST 9

Lessons 25 - 26 - 27

Go through this practice test without referring back to the last three lessons to see how many of the **boldface** words you can remember the signs for. After you have gone through the test go back over the lessons to check yourself.

1. My **elevators** work **off and on**; they never both work **at the same time**.

2. The **miserly** old man was very **selfish** in giving to the **needy**.

3. The **effect** of the heavy rainfall was the **overflowing** of the rivers and streams.

4. There was not **enough** money to **satisfy** her.

5. The police were very **harsh** on the **rebels**.

6. The young lady was easily **embarrassed**.

7. Do not **evade** the question!

8. It was with my **advice** that he applied for the job.

9. The baby was full of **awareness** at an early age.

10. It was a **relief** to know that John regained **consciousness**.

11. John tried to **conceive** the possible **effects** of the **strike**.

12. Can you juggle three balls **simultaneously**?

13. **Funerals** are not happy events.

14. I **noticed** that you filled out the **application**.

15. The old teacher was very **strict** and hard to **satisfy**.

16. The little boy felt **guilty** about having lied.

17. To keep a **charge** account requires **sufficient** money in the bank.

18. Did you **apply** pressure to the tourniquet?

19. Don't **back out from** the agreement **right away**.

20. The bull **charged** at the old man.

21. Don't **overlook** the importance of that **notice**.

22. Draft **evaders** are often full of **apprehension**.

LESSON 28

MIXED WORD GROUPS

allow — Use both hands; open "B" handshape, palms facing each other; move out in an upward curve.

permit — Use both hands; open "P" handshape; movement is the same as above.

fire — "flame".

fire (expel) — Use "S" handshape in left hand; hold with palm facing right; with the open "B" handshape in the right hand, palm up, mime sign chopping or cutting something off the "S".

like — Use one hand; open "8" handshape.

interesting — Use both hands; open "8" handshape the same as "like".

prefer, rather — Place hand on chest in the same initial position as you would in signing "enjoy"; move in the same way you would to sign "better" from the mouth.

hungry — Move "C" handshape only to stomach.

wish — Move same handshape only to lower chest.

desire — (1) Move same handshape only to lower chest with a stronger emphasis. (2) "want" with a stronger emphasis.

marry, marriage, married — Clasp hands together.

wedding — Join hands as in a handshake, but don't shake!

ticket — Use index and middle fingers; "punch" palm of opposite hand.

less — (1) meaning "reduce" in volume; sign as "reduce". (2) as in 'less than"; sign like "below".

agree (mentally) — Sign "agree" in the usual sense of agreeing with someone.

go with (agree in taste); appropriate; agreeable (in taste); becoming to, on; match (in color, agreement, etc.); fit (in taste) — Sign all these terms like "agree" except for placing one index finger to the chin instead of the forehead as in "agree" (mentally).

EXERCISES

Sign the following sentences, giving particular attention to the **boldface** words; fingerspell all words which cannot or should not be signed.

1. Karen's mother **allowed** her to have her ears pierced.

2. Donna **lets** her dog run free in the morning.

3. Sally **permits** her roommate to use her bicycle.

4. Did you see that **fire** last night?

5. Did you hear that Jack was **fired** this morning?

6. Larry **likes** Karen very much.

7. This is an **interesting** book.

8. I was very **hungry** by lunch time.

9. Johnny **wished** that he could have another bag of chips.

10. It was Kathy's **desire** to have a bigger house.

11. Their **marriage** took place in a garden.

12. Wasn't that a beautiful **wedding**?

13. Do you have a **ticket** for the show?

14. There was **less** gas in the car after the trip.

15. Scot gas costs **less than** Esso gas.

16. Her new dress **goes** very well **with** her hat.

17. The color scheme is very **appropriate** for today's new fashion.

18. The color scheme is **agreeable** with the rest of the house.

19. That new suit is **becoming** on her.

20. The color in her room **fits** the color in the hall.

21. Mr. Smith always **agrees** with Mr. Jones.

22. Would you **prefer** bowling or a movie tonight?

LESSON 29

MIXED WORD GROUPS

correct — (1) "right". (2) "to check for error as in grading". (3) "to criticize; to change or reform".

answer — Dbl. "1" handshape with index finger of R hand at lips - move out once.

reply, respond — Dbl. "R" handshape with "R" handshape of R hand at lips - move out once.

order, command — Use a more vigorous movement if you mean "command". Use only R hand.

invent, make up, devise — When these words refer to mental activity, use the "4" handshape, index finger at bottom of temple or forehead; slide up once.

draw, design, art — Use the little finger to trace a moving line down your left palm. For "design", <u>sign</u> like "draw" but use the "D" handshape. Use the "A" handshape for "art".

explain, explanation — Dbl. "F" handshape, palms facing each other; alternate back and forth.

describe, description, descriptive — Dbl. "D" handshape, palms facing each other; alternate back and forth. For **define**, use shorter movement.

back and forth — "Thumb up" handshape; move back and forth.

up and down — "Thumb up" handshape; move up and down.

bitter — Same as "sour".

disappoint (let down feeling) — Same sign used for "discouraged" as an Adj. Use open "8" handshape, fingers touching chest; slide fingers down.

to — (1) as an infinitive (to work; to study), always spell "t-o". (2) as a preposition (to town; to class), <u>sign</u> "to".

too — meaning "also" - <u>sign</u> like "same" or "alike".

create — (1) <u>Sign</u> like "invent" when referring to one's ability to think of original ideas. (2) <u>Sign</u> "make" when you mean a manual inference.

two — (number) - spell or sign.

too much — (concrete-abstract) - R hand fingers on top of left; raise R hand.

beat, defeat, conquer, overcome — Use dbl. "A" handshape, R wrist over left; move right "A" over and down.

beat, defeat, conquer — "shot H" movement; hold index and middle finger under thumb; release quickly into the "H" handshape.

last — (1) meaning "end of the line" - use the two little fingers, holding the left one out and striking across it with the right one. (2) meaning "the last one" - <u>sign</u> as above but hold left little finger down. (3) meaning "continue" - <u>sign</u> as in "stay" or "continue". (4) meaning "in the past" - <u>sign</u> "past".

EXERCISE 1

Sign the following sentences, giving particular attention to the **boldface** words; fingerspell all words which cannot or should not be signed.

1. Your answer is **correct**.

2. I must **correct** your papers.

3. How can we **correct** this situation?

4. **Answer** that letter today.

5. John's **reply** was very brief.

6. You should **respond** to one another.

7. I **ordered** my steak medium-rare.

8. The captain **commanded** attention.

9. Much **art** work is found on our old buildings.

10. Can you **draw** a picture of a horse?

11. Bob took **drafting** in college.

12. That **design** is beautiful.

13. The Smiths are **designing** their own home.

14. Who **invented** the telephone?

15. Can you **make up** a good story?

16. Bill will **devise** a plan for us.

17. **Create** your own title for this story.

18. Joyce is a very **creative** designer.

19. Please **explain** that sign again.

20. Signs are often very **descriptive.**

21. Mary **described** a beautiful sunset.

22. Find the right **definition** in the dictionary.

EXERCISE 2

Sign the following sentences, giving particular attention to the **boldface** words; fingerspell all words which cannot or should not be signed.

1. Do you drive **back and forth** to work?

2. My boy likes to go **up and down** in an elevator.

3. This seed tastes **bitter.**

4. John was **bitter** (very disappointed) about breaking up with his girl friend.

5. Are you **disappointed** in me?

6. I want **to** learn signs.

7. How far is it **to** Baltimore?

8. That answer is correct, **too.**

9. **Two** times **two** is not five!

10. John ate **too much** for lunch.

11. You talk **too much** somctimes.

12. Can you **beat** Jerry in ping pong?

13. Who **conquered** the British at Bunker Hill?

14. It is sometimes hard to **overcome** a bad cold.

15. The mob was **overcome** with tear gas.

16. That was the **last** time I saw the White House.

17. Being **last** in line is no fun.

18. **Last** night I had a bad dream!

19. How long does the movie **last**?

20. Who **designed** your new gown?

LESSON 30

SIGNING SONGS, POEMS OR HYMNS

In signing songs, poems or hymns, the deaf sign in such a way as to give the ideas in pictures and, at the same time attempt to preserve the beauty and rhythm of the music or meter of the song or poem. Words like "the" are usually omitted in the rendition of songs in the Language of Signs. With those words for which we have no sign, we must substitute with words which we can sign and which retain the appropriate meaning as closely as possible. This, in effect, is translating the idea into appropriate signs.

"AMERICA THE BEAUTIFUL"

Regular Version:

O, beautiful for spacious skies
For amber waves of grain
For purple mountain majesties
Above the fruited plain

America! America!
God shed His grace on thee
And crown thy good with brotherhood
From sea to shining sea!

Sign Language Version:

O, beautiful for (very large) skies
For (golden) waves. of (*) (growth)
For purple mountain (wonders)
(Over) (growing) ("land", flat or spreading)

America! America!
God (gave) His (blessing) on (you)
And crown (your) (good people) with (brother cooperation)
From sea to shining sea!

* "of" — possessive

"GOD BLESS AMERICA"

Regular Version:

God Bless America! Land that I love!
Stand beside her and guide her
Through the night with the light from above.
From the mountains to the prairies
To the oceans white with foam,
God Bless America! My home, sweet home.

94

Sign Language Version:

God Bless America! Land that I love!
Stand (near) her and (lead) her
Through night with light from above.
From mountains to ("land", flat or spreading)
To oceans white with (<u>mime sign</u> "foam")
God Bless America! My home, sweet home.

"THE STAR-SPANGLED BANNER"

Regular Version:

O, say can you see
By the dawn's early light
What so proudly we'd hailed
At the twilight's last gleaming
Whose broad stripes and bright stars
Through the perilous fight
O'er the ramparts we'd watched
Were still gallantly streaming
And the rocket's red glare,
The bombs bursting in air
Gave proof through the night
That our flag was still there!

O, say does that star-spangled banner yet wave
O'er the land of the free
And the home of the brave?

Sign Language Version:

O, (tell me) can you see
(Through) (<u>mime sign</u> "sunrise") light
What (so) proudly we'd hailed
(During) (sunset) last gleaming
Whose (big) stripes and bright stars
Through (terrible) (battle)
O'er (blockade) we'd watched
Were still (bravely) (waving back and forth)
And rocket's red ("bright" with strong emphasis)
(Explosions) in air
Gave proof through (all night)
That our flag still there!

O, say (?) that ** (still wave)
O'er land (*) free
And home (*) brave?
* "of" — possessive
** "star-spangled banner" — should be mime signed; that is, one literally draws a picture in the air indicating a small rectangular field of stars, a number of red and white stripes.

ramparts — Use dbl. "S" handshape; place one arm on top of the other and switch position of arms once as you move up and give the impression of a blockade.

rockets — Use "R" handshape on R hand and "C" on the L hand, L palm facing upward; push the "R" through the opening of L palm skyward; this represents a rocket being shot from a cannon. As you move skyward, allow "rocket" to explode.

glare — Sign "bright" twice with strong emphasis to give impression of a blinding light. [Turn head slightly away to give effect.]

bombs — Sign "explode" rapidly above head and repeat several times to indicate many bombs "bursting in air" all over the sky. [This takes care of the entire phrase "the bombs bursting in air".] [The "explosions" may be followed by clapping hands over ears for surrealistic effect.]

air — May simply sign "wind" or give R sweeping motion of the hands above head to indicate movement of air.

gallantly — Sign "brave".

streaming — Sign "waving" by holding R elbow in L palm and waving open hand ("5" handshape) vigorously back and forth.

proof — Use open dbl. "B" handshape [which means the letter "B" with thumbs protruding rather than turned inward]; hold L hand out with palm facing you and position the R hand the same way but close to the body; move R hand quickly out to come to rest on the L palm. [This indicates laying something down or out as evidence for anyone to see.]

spangled — [Literally this refers to a bright ornament decoration sewn on cloth. In signing "star spangled banner" a mime sign picture must be given. There are different versions, but I will explain the way I usually do it.]

1) Sign "star"; crook fingers using dbl. "5" handshape and move up literally "spattering" the stars in the sky.

"star"

"open "5" handshape — then move upward"

2) Hold "C" handshape on L hand in area of the "field of stars" and with the "C" on R hand "draw" a series of stripes out and down from the L hand, as in the flag.

3) With the dbl. "1" handshape fingers pointing towards each other "draw" the shape of a banner or flag in the air.

draw in the air

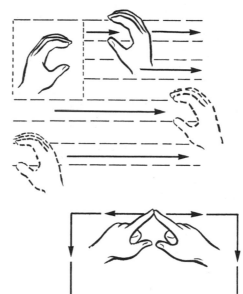

PRACTICE TEST 10

Lessons 28 - 29 - 30

Go through this practice test without referring back to the last three lessons to see how many of the **boldface** words you can remember the signs for. After you have gone through the test go back over the lessons to check yourself.

1. Which **answer** is the **correct** one?

2. Would you **permit** me to **correct** you on that?

3. Everyday most of us drive **back and forth** to work.

4. We must **respond** to a lot of **interesting** correspondence.

5. Would you **prefer** dancing or skating Saturday night?

6. It is Susie's **desire** to have a **wedding** in the woods.

7. Don't you **wish** we had **tickets** to the opera?

8. What did you **order** or are you **hungry**?

9. That wallpaper is a perfect **match** for your drapes.

10. The last **defeat** was **too disappointing**.

11. My design seems **less appropriate** than yours.

12. We were **disappointed** in John's **explanation**.

13. The **last** one does not always **last**.

14. **Last** night was **too much** for Henry!

15. Sometimes we all have a **desire** to **overcome** our limitations.

16. Once in a while we have a beautiful **sunset**.

17. Can you **describe** a **sunrise** over the ocean?

18. The **glare** of a car's headlights on high beam is bothersome.

19. I went **up and down** the stairs two times before I remembered what I wanted.

20. Are you going to major in **art** or **designing**?

21. I was **last** in a long, long line waiting to buy tags last March.

22. Have you **corrected** the **last** paper yet?

Part II

English Idioms
in
Sign Language

"Get up."

AN INTRODUCTION
TO
ENGLISH IDIOMS IN THE LANGUAGE OF SIGNS

The student who has completed and reviewed a basic course in the language of signs should be able to communicate fairly well with the deaf person who reads and writes good English. We shall define "good" English as the kind we would expect a typical hearing high school graduate to possess. The student will find, however, that the average deaf person, more likely than not, will have weak English and this will present an altogether different problem in communication. The average deaf person tends to sign much more than he will fingerspell. He also resorts to excessive use of pantomime. Part II and the ensuing Part III of this manual are, therefore, intended to help the student of the language of signs become more skilled in carrying on ordinary, informal conversations in sign language with the average deaf adult.

Part II consists of 15 lessons of English idioms translated into signs. The student is given a number of common idioms and their uses in each lesson and then shown how they would be signed. There is sufficient illustrative practice sentence material or exercises included at the end of each lesson in which all the idioms are in boldface. However, the instructor may wish to add illustrations and examples from time to time. He is free to do as he sees fit. Sometimes there is no sign for a given idiom. When this happens, the idea must be pantomimed in some way.

In this Part also, the student will meet three young ladies who are very much involved in things that happen. They are Jacqueline, Josephine, and Geraldine. The author would like to point out that the chief purpose of their inclusion is to provide additional practice and exercise for improving fingerspelling. It is hoped that the student will enjoy meeting and getting to know these ladies, but, more important, he should be able to spell names of such length with fluency.

Five Practice Tests are included, one after each three lessons. Their purpose is to provide the student with review material at reasonable intervals. These tests may be put on videotape for practice or given directly by the teacher in whatever order desired for additional receptive practice. The student may wish also to test himself by going over the sentences to see if he remembers the correct sign(s). He may then check himself by going back over the preceding lessons.

One point that should be stressed here is that, while the signs taught in Part II are acceptable for ordinary, informal conversations with the deaf in general, they should not be used to express idioms in schools and classes for deaf children. In a teaching situation, idiomatic expressions should be written or spelled out completely. Their translation into signs may be acceptable for purposes of expediency in defining them, but for no other reason. The student should understand, therefore, that Parts II and III are more concerned with helping him develop proficiency in manual communication with the deaf adult.

LESSON 1

Jacqueline   Josephine

"Take down the drapes."

1. **take a course** — <u>Sign</u>: "take up" (grasp something in both hands and pick it up)

2. **take up . . . golf** — <u>Sign</u>: "take up".
   . . . **a matter** — <u>Sign</u>: "discuss" <u>or</u> "take up .

3. **take on (as in hiring)** — <u>Sign</u>: accept" <u>or</u> you may use the sign for "admit" as in "welcome".

4. **take down . . . a picture, the drapes** — <u>Mime Sign</u>: "remove" followed by the object.
   . . . **notes** — <u>Sign</u>: "copy; write".
   . . . **a number** — <u>Sign</u>: "put down" in the sense of "jot down".

5. **take after . . . one's father in looks** — <u>Sign</u>: "look like".
   . . . **one's father in some skill** — <u>Sign</u>: "copy; imitate".

6. **take off . . . one's coat, hat, shoes, etc.** — <u>Mime Sign</u>: "remove" followed by the object.
   . . . **"as in an airplane took off"** — <u>Mime Sign</u>: a plane taking off.

7. **take out . . . the trash** — <u>Mime Sign</u>: carrying out a trash can.
   . . . **a friend** — <u>Mime Sign</u>: reach out, get a hold of an imaginary person, and pull him along with you.
   . . . **a book from the library** — <u>Mime Sign</u>: pick up an imaginary book from an imaginary shelf and remove it from the shelf.
   . . . **a word, sentence, or part** — <u>Sign</u>: "remove; eliminate; delete; or 'flick out'."

8. **take a walk** — <u>Sign</u>: "walking".

9. **take a seat** — <u>Sign</u>: "sit down".

10. **take turns** — Use "L" handshape; point to one person and then shift to the next, etc.

EXERCISES

Sign the following sentences, giving particular attention to the **boldface** English idioms; fingerspell all words which cannot or should not be signed.

1. Would you be interested in **taking** this sign language course?

2. Have you ever **taken up** bowling?

3. Please **take up** this matter with your lawyer. (<u>Sign</u>: "discuss")

4. Some employers refuse to **take on** any deaf workers.

5. **Take down** the curtains and wash them.

6. You should **take [down]** notes in each class.

7. The secretary **took down** every word the boss spoke.

8. Did you **take down** the license number of that car? (<u>Sign</u>: "put down")

9. Some children **take after** their fathers.

10. John **takes after** his father in his fishing skill.

11. **Take off** your coat and make yourself at home.

12. The huge jet **took off** after a 30-minute delay.

13. Geraldine **takes out** the trash on Tuesdays and Thursdays.

14. Each week Jacqueline **takes out** five books from the library.

15. Please **take out** line 2 of paragraph five in Section 1.

16. John **took** Josephine **out** for a date.

17. Will you **take a walk** with me to the library?

18. The professor told the young lady to please **take a seat**.

19. We will **take turns** in signing sentences in this practice lesson.

20. Let's **take** this lesson again, ok?

LESSON 2

1. **take hold of** — <u>Mime Sign</u>: holding something.

2. **take pity on** — <u>Sign</u>: "pity; sympathize".

3. **take sides** — <u>Sign</u>: "support".

4. **take a look at . . . something** — <u>Sign</u>: "look at".
   . . . **a problem or situation** — <u>Sign</u>: "investigate; check into".

5. **take apart** — <u>Mime Sign</u>: taking something apart.

6. **take part in . . . a play** — <u>Sign</u>: "act".
   . . . **track** — <u>Sign</u>: "complete" <u>or</u>, in this case, sign it literally.

7. **take time off** — <u>Sign</u>: "vacation".

8. **take over . . . for someone [take my place]** — <u>Sign</u>: "take up".
   . . . **a country** — <u>Sign</u>: "capture" with both hands.

9. **take it easy** — <u>Sign</u>: "rest" <u>or</u> "slow down" (may pantomime "holding back").

10. **try out . . . a game** — <u>Sign</u>: "try".
    . . . **a car** — "drive".
    . . . **for a play** — "volunteer".

11. **try on . . . a coat, a dress, a shirt, a hat, a blouse** — <u>Mime Sign</u>: trying on each article of clothing.

12. **think up . . . a story** — <u>Sign</u>: "make up" <u>or</u> "invent".
    . . . **a title**

13. **think of/about/over** — <u>Sign</u>: "think" + "about".

14. **turn on . . . the lights, the radio, the TV, the hi fi** — <u>Mime Sign</u>: the act of turning on each of these things.

15. **turn off . . . (all of the above)** — <u>Mime Sign</u>: the act of turning each of these off.

EXERCISES

Sign the following sentences, giving particular attention to the **boldface** English idioms; fingerspell all words which cannot or should not be signed.

1. Jacqueline screamed, "**Take hold of** the rope!"

2. We **take pity on** people who don't know what they want.

3. Do you often **take sides** in an argument?

4. Let's **take** a close **look at** this problem.

5. Jacqueline **took a look** at what was going on next door.

6. We will **take** this machine **apart**.

7. Jacqueline is interested in **taking part** in track.

8. Josephine will try to **take time** off from work.

9. Geraldine should **take over** for poor Josephine.

10. Russia tried to **take over** Poland.

11. We will **take it easy** for a while.

12. "**Take it easy,** buddy!"

13. Josephine wants to **try out** her new Mustang.

14. Jacqueline invited a few friends to **try out** a new game.

15. Jacqueline decided to **try out** for the fall play.

16. Would you like to **try on** this coat?

17. Josephine spent four hours **trying on** new hats.

18. Geraldine refused to **try on** a new mini-skirt.

19. She was recently **thrown out** of class for wearing a mini-skirt.

20. Can you **think up** a good title for this story?

LESSON 3

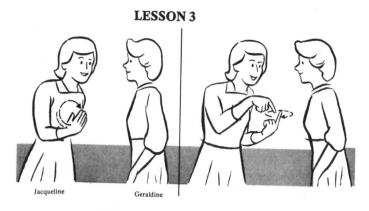

Jacqueline   Geraldine

"Please turn around!"

1. turn around — <u>Sign Hint</u>: Use Dbl. "1" handshape, fingers pointed up and down at each other; swing them around once.

2. turn out . . . new cars — <u>Sign</u>: "make" or <u>Mime Sign</u>: an assembly line.

3. turn down . . . someone — <u>Mime Sign</u>: Turn "thumbs down".

. . . **a radio/TV** — <u>Mime Sign</u>: the act of turning down the volume.

4. turn over (in a lying position) — <u>Sign Hint</u>: same as #1 except that you turn your fingers over in a "rolling position".

. . . **pancakes** — <u>Mime Sign</u>: Use hand as a spatula and turn as in turning pancakes over.

. . . **a new leaf** — <u>Sign</u>: "start again" <u>or</u> "start a new life".

5. throw out . . . of school — <u>Sign</u>: "throw out".

. . . **some pages** — <u>Sign</u>: "remove; eliminate" <u>or</u> <u>Mime Sign</u>: the flicking out

6. throw away — <u>Mime Sign</u>: whatever you are throwing away.

7. throw up — <u>Sign</u>: "vomit".

8. tear down . . . a building — <u>Sign</u>: "collapse" <u>or</u> "destroy" + "fall down".

9. tear up . . . a piece of paper — <u>Mime Sign</u>: tearing a piece of paper.

. . . **a room or a house** — <u>Sign</u>: "wreck" <u>or</u> "mess up".

10. used to . . . (as in "I used to do that") — <u>Sign</u>: "past" <u>or</u> "previously".

11. to be used to . . . (the weather) — <u>Sign</u>: "habit" + "to".

12. use your head — <u>Sign</u> this literally.

EXERCISES

Sign the following sentences, giving particular attention to the **boldface** English idioms; fingerspell all words which cannot or should not be signed.

1. Geraldine told Josephine to **turn around.**

2. That factory **turns out** thousands of TV sets each year.

3. Jacqueline was **turned down** for the new job.

4. Please **turn down** the radio so I can hear on the phone.

5. Geraldine decided to **turn over** a new leaf.

6. We will **throw out** all of the pages with errors on them.

7. Josephine said not to **throw away** any left-overs.

8. Geraldine **threw up** because she drank too much at the party Saturday.

9. Jacqueline watched a wrecking crew **tear down** an old mansion.

10. Over-exercising can **tear down** a person if he has not exercised regularly.

11. Josephine told Geraldine to **tear up** the note she wrote.

12. The robbers **tore up** the house.

13. Geraldine **used to** play the trombone while she was in school.

14. Jacqueline and Josephine **used to** perform in stage plays.

15. Will you ever **get used to** talking with your hands?

16. The teacher said, **"Use your head** to figure out that problem."

17. Our play was **turned down** for the tournament.

18. As it **turned out,** we didn't go to the seashore.

19. The road was **torn up** because of the flooding.

20. He **used to tear up** his old exams.

PRACTICE TEST 1

Lessons 1 - 2 - 3

Go through this practice test without referring back to the last three lessons to see how many of the **boldface** idioms you can remember signs for. After you have gone through the test go back over the lessons to check yourself.

1. Please **tear up** this note after you read it.

2. Would you like to **try out** my mini-bike?

3. **Take out** line 5 from paragraph 4.

4. Are you **used to** staying up late at night?

5. I need someone to **take over** for me for a while.

6. We must **take down** the drapes for cleaning.

7. My son likes to **take** things **apart** and put them together again.

8. I am trying to **think up** a good title for this poem.

9. We should **take turns** practicing in class.

10. It seems the weather **used to be** more stable than it is now.

11. **Turn on** the TV so we can get the news.

12. My friend **took me out** to dinner at The Flagship.

13. Do you always **take sides** in an argument?

14. Kennedy **turned down** McGovern's offer of the Vice-Presidency.

15. That old building will be **torn down** next year.

16. Did you **take** notes for me last night?

17. Please **think about** what I said.

18. Sometimes we **take pity** on very busy people.

19. Remember to **take it easy** on your vacation.

20. Would you like to **try on** this coat?

21. I am going to **take out** a book from the library.

22. Don't forget to **turn off** the lights when you leave.

LESSON 4

1. **get to . . . a place** — <u>Sign</u>: "arrive".

2. **get up . . . from bed or from a lying position** — <u>Mime Sign</u>: arising from a lying position.

3. **get up . . . from a chair or a seat** — <u>Mime Sign</u>: arising from a sitting position.

4. **get down** — <u>Mime Sign</u>: the act of getting down.

5. **get away** — <u>Sign</u>: "leave"; (for "getaway" <u>Sign</u>: "escape.)

6. **get away with** — <u>Sign</u> this literally or <u>sign</u> "do". May <u>sign</u> "avoid" if you mean "get away with" in the sense of keeping from doing what you should.

7. **get sick** — <u>Sign</u>: "become" + "sick".

8. **get stuck (or be stuck)** — <u>Sign</u>: "become" + "stuck".

9. **get over . . . the mumps** — <u>Sign</u>: "become well" <u>or</u> "finish with". May be signed literally as in: "I can't get over this."

10. **get on . . . a horse, a fence, a plane, train, bus, etc.** — <u>Mime Sign</u>: the act of getting on or in.

11. **get off . . . each of these things** — <u>Mime Sign</u>: the action in reverse.

12. **get out of . . . a car, train, bus; of here** — <u>Sign Hint</u>: same as "get off" a car, train, bus.

    . . . as an expression — <u>Mime Sign</u>: use gesture.

13. **get along with** — <u>Sign</u>: "proceed" or "go ahead" + "with".

14. **get back from . . . a trip** — <u>Sign</u>: "arrive" + "from".

15. **get better** — <u>Sign</u>: "improve".

    . . . worse — <u>Sign</u>: "regress" <u>or</u> opposite of "improve".

16. **get used to . . . (someone or something)** — <u>Sign</u>: "become" + "habit" + "to".

17. **get rid of** — May <u>sign</u> "remove" or <u>Mime Sign</u> by brushing your R hand off the L hand in a sweeping motion.

EXERCISES

Sign the following sentences, giving particular attention to the **boldface** English idioms; fingerspell all words which cannot or should not be signed.

1. When will this train **get to** Chicago?

2. Geraldine has a hard time **getting up** in the morning.

3. You should **get up** when the President enters the room.

4. I **got stuck** in a snowdrift last winter.

5. Some students try to **get away** with doing very little work.

6. Geraldine saw Jacqueline up in a tree and screamed: **Get down** from there!"

7. We all need to "**get away**" from it all at times.

8. Draft dodgers think they can **get away** with burning their draft cards.

9. Geraldine **got sick** last week from eating too many sweets.

10. Jacqueline **got tired** from driving so long.

11. When do you expect to **get over** the measles?

12. Let's **get on** a train and go to New York tomorrow.

13. The three ladies went riding one day, but Josephine refused to **get on** her horse.

14. The officer told Jacqueline to **get in** her car and follow him.

15. The children were told to **get off** the fence.

16. Sometimes it is difficult for some people to **get along** with one another.

17. When did you **get back** from your trip?

18. The patient slowly **got better** after surgery; then he suddenly **got worse**.

19. The Salvation Army asks people to **get rid of** unused clothing.

20. There are many cats and dogs that do not **get along**.

21. Please **get out of** here now!

22. We must **get down** to see you soon.

109

LESSON 5

1. get on one's nerves — May rephrase this to read: "make one nervous" or <u>sign</u> it literally as many deaf do.

2. get even with — <u>Sign</u>: "revenge" <u>or</u> "get equal or level with".

3. look up . . . something — <u>Mime Sign</u>: thumbing through the pages.
   . . . at something — <u>Sign</u>: "look", but move fingers up.

4. look down on — <u>Sign</u>: "look", moving fingers down, then sign "on".

5. look up to — <u>Sign</u>: "look", moving fingers up, then sign "to".

6. look after — <u>Sign</u>: "supervise" <u>or</u> "take care of".

7. look over . . . a report — <u>Sign</u>: "read", indicating what you want to look over.
   . . . a car — <u>Mime Sign</u>: looking around + car.

8. look into — <u>Sign</u>: "investigate" <u>or</u> "check into".

9. look forward to — <u>Sign</u>: "look" with both hands moving forward in 2 movements.

10. look at (or take a look at) — <u>Sign</u>: "look", pointing with the "eyes" to the object to be seen.

11. look away — <u>Sign</u>: "look", moving away from an object or person, whichever it happens to be.

12. go with — Can be <u>signed</u> literally as in: "I will <u>go with</u> Jim."
   Can be <u>signed</u> like "to go steady", <u>signing</u> "with" repeatedly.
   Can be <u>signed</u> "agree with" (in taste) as in: "that hat doesn't <u>go with</u> that coat."

13. go on — May be <u>signed</u> "continue".
   May be <u>signed</u> "proceed" as with "get along".
   May be <u>signed</u> literally as in: "We will go on a trip."

14. go out — <u>Sign</u>: "fade" <u>or</u> "vanish" as in: "The fire went out."

EXERCISES

Sign the following sentences, giving particular attention to the **boldface** English idioms; fingerspell all words which cannot or should not be signed.

1. Does your boss sometimes **get on your nerves**?

2. Geraldine does not believe in **getting even** with anyone.

3. Josephine loves to **look up** at the stars at night.

4. Will you **look after** my house while I am gone to New York?

5. Students often **look up** to certain professors as their ideals.

6. One must **look after** his bills each month. (Sign: "take care of" or "pay attention to")

7. **Look up** the word if you are not sure of its origin.

8. Do you ever **look down on** anyone?

9. **Look up at** that crazy airplane!

10. Come and **take a look** at this strange bug!

11. When Josephine scolded Geraldine for looking at her mail, Geraldine shamefully **looked away**.

12. **Look over** the samples and see if there are any you like best.

13. The boss told Jacqueline to **look over** her papers carefully to be sure none were missing.

14. The fire **went out** slowly because no one had tended it.

15. Please **look into** this matter as soon as you can.

16. Are you **looking forward** to the next sign language course?

17. Geraldine was told that her new blouse did not **go well** with her skirt.

18. Jacqueline has been **going with** Nicholas for two years now.

19. **Go on** with your work as you planned.

20. Suddenly, the lights **went out**.

LESSON 6

1. **go out with ... someone** — May be <u>signed</u> literally or the <u>sign</u> "gone" may be used.

2. **go down to** — <u>Sign</u>: "go" as in going down from one point to another.

3. **go over ... a paper** — <u>Sign</u>: "look or read over", as with a paper or a report.
   ... to someone's place — <u>Sign</u>: "go" as in "going over" to the neighbors.

4. **go in for** — <u>Sign</u>: "interest in" or "eager in" (here rub hands together to show eagerness).

5. **go away** — <u>Sign</u>: literally as in: "We are going away."
   <u>Sign</u>: "fade" or "vanish" or "disappear" as in "It will soon go away."
   <u>Sign</u>: like "get away from here!" (scram or shoo!)

6. **go wrong** — <u>Sign</u>: "happen" as in "What went wrong?"

7. **go up to** — <u>Sign</u>: "approach" or "meet" without actually meeting. (Use dbl. "1" handshape.)

   <u>Sign</u>: "go up" literally, and <u>sign</u> "to".

8. **come across ... an old friend** — <u>Sign</u>: "meet".
   ... a lost dollar — <u>Sign</u>: "find".

9. **come about** — <u>Sign</u>: "happen".

10. **come true** — May be <u>signed</u> literally <u>or</u> sign "become true".

11. **come to** — <u>Sign</u>: "awake" as from a fainting spell <u>or</u> a knockout.

12. **come over** — <u>Sign</u>: "come" and "over" literally.

13. **come up to** — <u>Sign</u>: the same as "go up to", (Number 7, movement is toward self).

EXERCISES

Sign the following sentences, giving particular attention to the **boldface** English idioms; fingerspell all words which cannot or should not be signed.

1. With whom did Josephine **go out** last Saturday?

2. Josephine decided to **go out with** a friend.

3. **Go down** to the store and get a bottle of aspirin, please.

4. **Go over** these plans with me to see if they are correct.

5. Let's **go over** to Geraldine's apartment tonight.

6. Do you **go in for** this type of gambling?

7. I thought the growling dog would **go away** if I ignored it.

8. I wish this bad dream would **go away**!

9. I heard the meeting was cancelled last night. What **went wrong**?

10. Something **went wrong** with the missile launch.

11. Jacqueline **came across** an old friend at the dance.

12. How did that accident **come about**?

13. Will your dreams ever **come true**?

14. The boxer, after being knocked out, finally **came to**.

15. **Come over** sometime and visit with me.

16. Please **come up** to the office sometime.

17. To my surprise, I **came across** a five dollar bill in my pocket.

18. What's **wrong** with you today?

19. **Go away** from the water's edge!

20. I could **go in for** a delicious steak!

PRACTICE TEST 2

Lessons 4 - 5 - 6

Go through this practice test without referring back to the last three lessons to see how many of the **boldface** idioms you can remember the signs for. After you have gone through the test go back over the lessons to check yourself.

1. **Come over** to my house after the game. O.K.?

2. I **got off** the Metro at Capital Beltway.

3. Most of us **look forward to** vacation time.

4. **With** whom did you **go out** last Saturday?

5. When do you expect to **get back from** New York?

6. Will you please **go over** my report for me?

7. Please **go on** with your story, Jack.

8. It is hard to **get up** on some mornings.

9. A drunk **came up** to me on the street and mumbled something.

10. Maybe we should **look up** this word to be sure.

11. Sometimes a bad cold **gets worse** before it **gets better**.

12. I don't know what **went wrong** with my car.

13. Sometimes we wish our problems would just **go away**.

14. Our train should **get to** Philadelphia by 10:05.

15. The other day I **came across** a picture of my former sweetheart.

16. People don't **look down on** other people in trouble as they **used to**.

17. I don't think that tie **goes with** that suit.

18. If this **gets on your nerves**, just **look away** for a minute.

19. We hope our dream of **going away** to Europe **comes true**.

20. "I must **go down to** the sea again" is a beautiful poem.

21. Please **look at** me while I explain the situation.

22. It's not easy to **get rid of** crabgrass.

Geraldine   Jacqueline   Josephine

"You've put on weight."

1. **put on . . . a hat, coat, etc.** — <u>Mime Sign</u>: the act of putting these on.

 . . . a show — <u>Sign</u>: "give" + "a show".

 . . . an act — <u>Sign</u>: "pretend" or "fool". Use "A" handshape on R hand; "1" on L hand, "knock on" the "1" two or three times.

2. **put off** — <u>Sign</u>: "postpone".

3. **put out . . . your cigarette** — <u>Mime Sign</u>: crushing out a cigarette.

 . . . the lights — <u>Sign</u>: "turn off the lights"; also may apply to "put out the fire".

4. **put up** — <u>Sign</u>: "make", "build", <u>or</u> "set up" — same as "establish".

 . . . signs — <u>Mime Sign</u>: the act of posting <u>or</u> putting up the sign.

5. **put up with** — <u>Sign</u>: "patience" two ways. (These signs also mean "can't stand" or "bear <u>with</u>"; of course, <u>sign</u> "can't" first).

6. **put on weight** — <u>Sign</u>: "increase" + "weight".

7. **put together** — <u>Mime Sign</u>: putting something together opposite of "take apart".

8. **put down** — <u>Sign</u>: "suppress". Use "Open-B" handshape on R hand; push down the "1". This would be a sort of "pushover".

 . . . the answer, note — <u>Sign</u>: "write" or "jot down".

 . . . that knife — <u>Mime Sign</u>: the act of putting the object down.

9. **put down . . . on a purchase** — Use "C" handshape on L palm; move "C" down from the palm.

 pay cash for . . . something — <u>Sign</u>: the same as above, but move "C" out instead of down.

115

10. **be up to** — Use sign language idiom "think-self" for "It is up to you to decide." Sign: "depend on" for "It is up to you whether we go."

11. **up to something** — Sign: "do" with a suspicious expression. In the negative sense, "I am not up to this today", sign: "don't feel like doing".

12. **shut up** — Mime Sign: the expression "Shut up!" In the sense of being "shut in", use the dbl. "2" handshape to indicate being "imprisoned" or sign: "stay"

13. **stir up . . . trouble** — Sign: "make" or "cause".
    . . . a cake — Mime Sign: the stirring action.

14. **catch up . . . with someone** — Form "chase" sign; then close in, moving only **. . . with something** the R hand.

15. **pick up . . . something** — Sign: "take up" (one hand only).
    . . . where you left off — Sign: "start" or "begin".
    . . . someone — Often signed literally, using the sign "pick up" made with the thumb and index finger.

16. **stick up** — (Meaning a "hold up") Mime Sign the act of aiming 2 guns, then sign "steal".
    As in "His hair sticks up funny", mime sign.

17. **hang up . . . the phone, the coat** — In either case, mime sign the action indicated.

EXERCISES

Sign the following sentences, giving particular attention to the **boldface** English idioms; fingerspell all words which cannot or should not be signed.

1. **Put on** your best clothes for the party.

2. The children **put on** a puppet show for us.

3. It is hard to **put on** a good act when one is guilty.

4. Let's not **put off** writing this report.

5. Please **put out** your cigarette before you burn something.

6. **Put out** the lights before leaving the room.

7. Geraldine **put up** the card table for the game.

8. Josephine is a slow typist. Please **put up** with her.

9. Eating cookies is a good way to **put on weight**.

10. Let's **put together** the puzzle, "We and They".

11. **Put down** the answer to this question.

12. Josephine **put down** $500.00 on her new car.

13. I prefer to **pay cash for** most things I buy.

14. I know Jacqueline and Jerry must be **up to something.**

15. Plants should not be **shut up** in a dark room.

16. Let's **stir up** some excitement in this place!

17. I will try to **catch up** on my sleep this weekend.

18. Please **pick up** the book from the floor.

19. **Pick up** your conversation where you left off.

20. There were three **stick-ups** on 14th Street last night.

21. At your cowlick, your hair **sticks up** very oddly.

22. "**Hang up** the phone before you spend all my money!"

Jacqueline   Josephine

"I stayed up all night."

1. **show up, come up, pop up** — <u>Sign</u>: reverse of "disappear"; bring right index finger up between left index and middle fingers.
2. **stay up** — <u>Sign</u>: "awake" with dbl. "C" handshape.

3. **keep up** — <u>Sign</u>: "continue" <u>or</u> "stay with" <u>or</u> <u>sign</u> as "keep" and spell "up" (Coll).
4. **time is up** — Use <u>sign</u> language idiom: "time finished" or simply "finish", shaking both hands simultaneously.

5. **blow up** — <u>Sign</u>: "explode" for literally blowing up something.

   Meaning "to lose one's temper", <u>sign</u> "blow one's top", using "S" handshape on L hand, palm facing right, and "5" or "Open-B" handshape on L; move up and down, wiggling hand as you do.
6. **bring up . . . children** — <u>Sign</u>: "grow up" or "raise".

   . . . an idea — <u>Sign</u>: "suggest".

7. **stand up** — For "arise", <u>sign</u> the same as "get up".

   As in "Will these tires stand up under hard driving?" <u>Sign</u>: "continue" or "last".

   As in "She stood up her date", rephrase the statement to: "She didn't show up" or "She refused to go with him."

8. **hold up . . . business** — <u>Sign</u>: "suspend".

   . . . the fish you caught — <u>Mime Sign</u>: holding up the fish.

   . . . a store — Meaning "to rob", <u>mime sign</u> holding a pistol; then sign "rob" <u>or</u> "steal".
9. **make up . . . for lost time** — <u>Sign</u>: literally.

   . . . an excuse — <u>Sign</u>: "invent".

   . . . and be friends — <u>Sign</u>: literally.

   . . . one's face — <u>Mime Sign</u>: putting make-up on the face.

118

10. **draw up . . . a contract** — <u>Sign</u>: "prepare".

     . . . a chair — <u>Sign</u>: "come, sit down".

11. **let up** — <u>Sign</u>: "lessen" (less) in the sense of reducing in amount <u>or</u> "stop" if it means that.

12. **back one up** — <u>Sign</u>: "support".

13. **back up . . . the car** — (You know this one!) Use "3" handshape for the car; move backwards.

     As in: "Traffic is backed up for 2 miles!", use dbl. "3" handshape; hold one hand still and move the other back to represent many cars lined up.

14. **back out . . . from a commitment** — <u>Sign</u>: "avoid".

     . . . the car — <u>Mime Sign</u>: as in #13.

     As in "I'll be back out someday.", <u>sign</u> "return" or "come back".

15. **buy up** — <u>Sign</u>: "buy", repeating the movement quickly several times.

EXERCISES

Sign the following sentences, giving particular attention to the **boldface** English idioms; fingerspell all words which cannot or should not be signed.

1. The President **showed up** unexpectedly at the Gallaudet Commencement last June.

2. Do you think this problem will **come up** again?

3. Many students **stay up** all night to cram for exams.

4. The boss told Geraldine to **keep up** with the good work.

5. Josephine had almost finished the exam when the **time was up!**

6. The mine **blew up** suddenly and without warning!

7. Jacqueline **blew her stack** over such a little incident!

8. How many children have you **brought up?**

9. Geraldine suggested that Josephine **bring up** another idea.

10. "**Stand up** and be counted!" (<u>Sign</u> "stand" emphatically)

11. I don't know if these old tires will **stand up** much longer.

12. Business was **held up** because the banks were closed.

13. **Hold up** the fish you caught so I can take a picture.

14. Do we have any **make up** classes?

15. In the theatre, it is necessary to **make up** carefully.

16. Has the wind **let up** yet?

17. Josephine decided to **back out** from the committee work.

18. **Back up** so I can check that tire.

19. Will you **back** Josephine for President of the Ladies' Guild?

20. Don't **buy up** all the eggs in the store!

LESSON 9

1. **hold on . . . to something** — <u>Mime Sign</u>: holding onto something.
   . . . for a minute — <u>Sign</u>: "suspend".

2. **hold off** — <u>Sign</u>: "postpone".

3. **hold out** — <u>Sign</u>: "continue" <u>or</u> "last" in the sense of staying on.

4. **hold over** — <u>Sign</u>: "postpone", extending only one hand out.

5. **hold still** — Usually "keep quiet" will do for this.

6. **make believe, pretend** — <u>Sign</u>: "pretend" in the sense of "fooling" or <u>sign</u> literally.

7. **make sure** — <u>Sign</u>: "make true".

8. **make out . . . a will** — <u>Sign</u>: "make" only leave off "out".
   . . . on a test — <u>Sign</u>: "do".
   . . . in college — <u>Sign</u>: "do" <u>or</u> "succeed".
   Sometimes signed like "work out", you "mesh gears" with your hands.

9. **make good . . . money** — <u>Sign</u>: literally.
   . . . in something — <u>Sign</u>: "succeed" or "do good".

10. **make up one's mind** — Can be <u>signed</u> literally or sometimes signed "decide".

11. **make faces** — <u>Sign</u>: "expression" (facial type, of course).

12. **cut out** — <u>Mime Sign</u>: cutting something with a pair of scissors.
   Cut that out! — <u>Sign</u>: "stop that".

13. **carry out . . . something** — <u>Mime Sign</u>: carrying something out.
   . . . a plan, an order — <u>Sign</u>: "follow" <u>or</u> "obey".

14. **fill out . . . a report or an application** — <u>Sign</u>: "answer" several times in a row <u>or</u> "put down" in order.

15. **keep out, keep off** — <u>Sign</u>: "stay out" <u>or</u> "stay off" (fingerspell "off").

EXERCISES

Sign the following sentences, giving particular attention to the **boldface** English idioms; fingerspell all words which cannot or should not be signed.

1. **Hold on** a minute until I finish this call!

2. **Hold on**to my hand so you won't get lost.

3. **Hold your horses**! We'll come to that part soon! (<u>Sign</u> "wait" 2 or 3 times)

4. We had better **hold off** the party until next month.

5. I hope we can **hold out** until next spring!

6. The show was **held over** for 2 full weeks!

7. Jacqueline told Geraldine to please **hold still** while she was putting up her hair.

8. I'll be **back out** for a longer visit next month.

9. Disneyland is supposed to be a "Land of **Make-Believe**".

10. **Make sure** you know which sign to use with the bold face words in this lesson.

11. How do you think we will **make out** by the end of this course?

12. Can you **make out** what the announcer is saying? (<u>Sign</u> "understand")

13. Josephine **made out** an application for a loan and forgot to sign her name.

15. Geraldine didn't **make out** very well in college so she withdrew.

16. **Make up your mind** so we can continue!

17. The professor said: "**Cut out** that joking and get to work!"

18. Josephine is **cutting out** a new dress now.

19. Please help me **carry out** this box of books.

20. Now remember, **carry out** this plan very carefully.

21. Please **fill out** this form carefully.

22. The sign says: "**KEEP OUT** — DANGER!"

PRACTICE TEST 3

Lessons 7 - 8 - 9

Go through this practice test without referring back to the last three lessons to see how many of the **boldface** idioms you can remember the signs for. After you have gone through the test go back over the lessons to check yourself.

1. We were **held up** in traffic and didn't **show up** on time.

2. **Make sure** you **fill out** the application accurately.

3. We will **put off** this lesson until next week; **time is up**.

4. That movie was **held over** for two weeks.

5. We had to **put up with** the rain because it wouldn't **let up**.

6. When I quit smoking I **put on** a lot of weight.

7. **Hold still** while I finish your **make up**.

8. I had to run to **catch up with** Bob.

9. Have you **made up your mind** about going with us?

10. How much should I **put down** on a new car?

11. Please **bring up** your idea at the meeting, O.K.?

12. Will you help me **carry out** the garbage?

13. Please **hold on a minute** while I **back** the car **out**.

14. My dad **blew up** because we wouldn't **cut out** the nonsense.

15. Someone **bought up** all the bread in the store.

16. Don't **stay up** all night just for me!

17. A storm **came up** and **kept up** all night.

18. Don't **make up** excuses about not **being up** to working.

19. Let's **put up** a sign to advertise our party.

20. I think Jerry was just **putting on an act**.

21. If you have agreed to help, please don't **back out** now!

22. Did you read about the big **hold up**?

123

LESSON 10

1. **knock out** — <u>Sign</u>: "K.O."; "T.K.O." for "technical knockout".

2. **leave out** — <u>Sign</u>: "forget" for "leaving out" in the sense of forgetting.
   <u>Sign</u>: "remove" for "leave out" in the sense of taking away or deleting.

3. **pick out** — <u>Sign</u>: "choose".

4. **point out** — <u>Sign</u>: "show".

5. **run out of** — <u>Sign</u>: "use up" (Sign language idiom "all gone"; L hand index finger pointing out; R hand "5" on base of L index finger; slide out to an "S").

6. **set out . . . a plant** — <u>Sign</u>: "put out".
   . . . for some place — <u>Sign</u>: "start" <u>or</u> "begin" <u>or</u> "leave".

7. **stand out** — <u>Sign</u>: "notice" (noticeable) As in "He <u>stood out</u> in the crowd."
   <u>Sign</u>: "appear", moving around in a circle.

8. **strike out . . . in baseball** — <u>Sign</u>: "K", striking the L palm.
   . . . a word or sentence — <u>Sign</u>: "cross out", "eliminate" <u>or</u> "take out".

9. **work out** — <u>Sign</u>: "practice" for "work out in football".
   <u>Sign</u> "machine", meshing gears only once for "All <u>worked out</u> fine!"
   Can use "succeed".

10. **keep** — As in "The cold kept me from enjoying myself." <u>Sign</u>: "prevent" for "keep".

11. **break out . . . with a rash** — <u>Mime Sign</u>: spots all over the face and body.
    . . . of jail — <u>Sign</u>: "escape".
    . . . as a "fire broke out" — <u>Sign</u>: "start".
    . . . as in "An epidemic breaking out" — <u>Sign</u>: "spread".

12. **break down** — Usually "break" will suffice.
    <u>Sign</u>: "breakdown" (new) like "fall" <u>or</u> "collapse".

13. **break through** — <u>Sign</u> literally <u>or</u> <u>sign</u> "make a new discovery" if it is used in that sense.

14. **break away** — <u>Sign</u>: "escape" <u>or</u> "disjoin" as in breaking loose from something.

EXERCISES

Sign the following sentences, giving particular attention to the **boldface** English idioms; fingerspell all words which cannot or should not be signed.

1. Patterson was **knocked out** by Liston in the big fight.

2. The party was a **knock out**! (<u>Sign</u> "success")

3. Please **leave out** any unnecessary information.

4. Geraldine felt **left out** at the big party. (<u>Sign</u> literally or "alone")

5. **Pick out** the dog you like best.

6. Will you **point out** the way for me?

7. Imagine! Geraldine **ran out** of food before payday!

8. The weather was beautiful when we **set out** on our trip South.

9. We **set out** five azalea plants last spring.

10. Jacqueline really **stood out** in the crowd because of her height. (<u>Sign</u> "was noticed")

11. Poor Casey **struck out** just when all the bases were full!

12. Please **strike out** sentence 3 in paragraph 4.

13. How often do you **work out**? (<u>Sign</u> "exercise")

14. Everything **worked out** just fine for Jacqueline.

15. Basketball players must **work out** daily. (<u>Sign</u> "practice")

16. A bad cold **kept** Josephine from going to the dance.

17. Sally **broke out** with a heat rash.

18. The three men tried to **break out** of jail.

19. The fire **broke out** on the second floor of the house.

20. My car **broke down** on the highway.

21. There are always new **break throughs** in cancer research.

22. Going up a hill, the trailer **broke away** from the car.

125

1. **drop in on** — Sign: "visit" or "pop up for a visit".

2. **drop out** — Sign: "quit" or simply let R hand drop out of L hand for a school dropout.

3. **fall through** — Sign: "collapse" similar to "breakdown".

4. **fall behind** — Sign: similarly to "avoid", but let rear hand actually fall back.

5. **fall off** — Sign: literally.
   Sign: "lessen" if in the sense of reducing.

6. **every so often, now and then, from time to time, once in a while, etc.** — Use the open "B" handshape move forward in a series of slight jumps at different speeds to indicate time variations.

7. **pay attention to** — Sign: "attention"; whether movement is out from you or in toward you depends on what you're calling attention to.

8. **right away; at once** — Sign: "now" with emphasis or sign "fast".

9. **as usual** — Sign: "as"; then add "since", "up to now", or "all along" (same as for "been").

10. **by oneself** — Sign: "alone".

11. **to call on . . . someone** — Sign: "visit".
    . . . someone to do something — Sign: "beckon" or "call" in that sense.

12. **lie down** — Sign: "legs", actually in a lying position on L palm.

13. **so far** — Sign: the same as "been".

14. **shake hands** — Clasp hands and shake them.

15. **call off** — Sign: "cancel" or "cross out".

16. **for good** — Sign: "continue" or "always", followed by "continue".

EXERCISES

Sign the following sentences, giving particular attention to the **boldface** English idioms; fingerspell all words which cannot or should not be signed.

1. Jacqueline and her husband **dropped in on** Josephine and Geraldine last Sunday.

2. Jack **dropped out** of the club without paying his dues.

3. The problem of school **dropouts** continues to bother many school administrators.

4. We hope our plans for landing a man on the moon in 1969 don't **fall through**.

5. Don't **fall behind** in your studies!

6. Geraldine **fell off** the porch yesterday and sprained her ankle.

7. Prices on many products have not **fallen off** in years!

8. **Every so often** you hear a complaint about Washington's weather.

9. We get snow here **once in a while** during the winter.

10. **From time to time**, Josephine joins a health club to try to keep her figure.

11. The professor said, "Now, **pay attention** to this!"

12. How often do you **pay attention to** your sign lessons?

13. Will you go to the store **right away** and get me a loaf of bread?

14. The weather here is fickle **as usual**.

15. Please **call on** me if you need any help.

16. You are always welcome **to call on** us anytime.

17. **Lie down** and rest a few minutes and you will feel better!

18. Do you enjoy working **by yourself**?

19. **So far**, we have made good progress in this course.

20. Let's **shake hands** and be friends again. O.K.?

21. The meeting will be **called off** if no one else shows up.

22. Do you plan to stay in Washington **for good**? (<u>Sign</u> "always")

Jacqueline   Josephine

"I fell in love with Jim."

1. **count on** — <u>Sign</u>: "depend on".

2. **out-of-order . . . a machine** — In most cases, "broke" will do.
   . . . a telephone — <u>Sign</u>: "not working".
   . . . a room — <u>Sign</u>: "messed up" — also fingerspelled.

3. **at times** — <u>Sign</u>: "sometimes" <u>or</u> "occasionally".

4. **keep on** — <u>Sign</u>: "continue".

5. **to be over** — <u>Sign</u>: "finished".

6. **by the way** — <u>Sign</u>: "change the subject" <u>or</u> fingerspell it literally. For "subject", <u>sign</u> quotation marks.

7. **over and over** — <u>Sign</u>: "again and again".

8. **fall in love with** — <u>Sign</u>: this literally or use the sign language idiom associated with this. (Use "1" handshape on R-hand, placing tip of index finger at tip of nose; hold L-hand out in "5" handshape; bring the "1" down to L-palm rather vigorously.)

9. **as yet** — <u>Sign</u>: "since" (been).

10. **to have to do with** — <u>Sign</u>: "have" possessively, fingerspell "do"; <u>or</u> substitute "connect" (related) for do and add "with".

11. **to be in charge of, to have charge of** — <u>Sign</u>: "control" <u>or</u> "manage" <u>or</u> "administer" <u>or</u> "responsible", depending upon the intent.

12. **quite a few** — <u>Sign</u>: "several" <u>or</u> "many", depending on intention.

13. **find fault with** — <u>Sign</u>: "mistake" for fault or <u>Sign</u>: "blame" <u>or</u> "criticize" as a substitute for the whole expression.

128

14. **it's up to you** — Sign: literally <u>or</u> use the sign language idiom, "think-self".

15. **keep track of** — Mime <u>Sign</u>: putting items on a list <u>or</u> <u>Sign</u>: "follow around".

EXERCISES

Sign the following sentences, giving particular attention to the **boldface** English idioms; fingerspell all words which cannot or should not be signed.

1. Can we **count on** you to be present?

2. This room is completely **out of order**! (<u>Sign</u> "messed up")

3. The jukebox was **out of order** yesterday. (<u>Sign</u> "broken")

4. Sorry, but that phone is **out of order**. (<u>Sign</u> "not working")

5. **At times**, it is hard to keep up with all the work one must do.

6. **Keep on** trying and do the best you can.

7. After the show **was over**, we went to the Hot Shoppes for a snack.

8. **By the way**, what do you think of this plan?

9. Practice your signs **over and over** and you will remember them.

10. Josephine gets tired of telling the same stories **over and over**.

11. Geraldine **fell in love with** Jim at first sight.

12. **As yet**, we have not decided who should win the prize. (trophy for prize)

13. Jacqueline will **have nothing to do with** troublemakers!

14. Miss Nannybrook **has charge of** the exams this week. (<u>Sign</u> "give out")

15. Who is **in charge of** the jukebox?

16. Are you **in charge of** the decorations committee?

17. **Quite a few** people are interested in sign language now.

18. Jacqueline is always **finding fault with** Josephine and Geraldine.

19. It is really **up to you** whether we go or not. (<u>Sign</u> "depend on")

20. If you want to join, **it's up to you.**

129

PRACTICE TEST 4

Lessons 10 - 11 - 12

Go through this practice test without referring back to the last three lessons to see how many of the **boldface** idioms you can remember the signs for. After you have gone through the test go back over the lessons to check yourself.

1. **Once in a while** I **fall behind** in my work.

2. Unless things **work out**, we will have to **call off** the party.

3. Don't try **to find fault with** Bill; everyone makes mistakes.

4. I have told you **over and over** to **lie down**.

5. Can you **keep track of** the scores **by yourself**?

6. **As usual** the coke machine is **out of order**.

7. Please **call on me** if you need help, O.K.?

8. Can you **point out** the car you **picked out**?

9. Our plans to **drop in on** you **fell through** at the last minute.

10. May we **count on** you to come right away if we **call**?

11. The show **was** just about **over** when a fire **broke out**.

12. Joe is **in charge of quite a few** special events.

13. Judy **broke down** and cried when her cat **broke away**.

14. Marge was embarrassed because she **ran out of** sugar while serving coffee.

15. Bad weather **kept** us from **calling on** the Blistenstips.

16. Please **pay attention to** your **workout**; don't overdo it.

17. We will **set out** for the Great Falls hike Friday at 5:00 a.m.

18. **Keep on** arguing and I will go mad!

19. **Leave out** the word "parasite" and the paragraph will be O.K.

20. **At times** we **fall in love with** someone too easily.

21. Please **keep track of** all the supplies on hand.

22. Do you always **set out** new plants in the spring?

130

LESSON 13

1. call down — <u>Sign</u>: "bawl out" (sign language idiom, made with the Dbl. "S" handshape; one "S" in front of the other and placed in front of forehead; move out and let go into a Dbl. "C" handshape, hands apart.)

2. do over — <u>Sign</u>: "do again".

3. feel sorry for — <u>Sign</u>: literally <u>or</u> <u>sign</u> "pity" <u>or</u> "sympathize" + "for".

4. become of — <u>Sign</u>: "happen to".

5. to play tricks on — <u>Sign</u>: "fool" (in sense of pretend).
<u>Sign</u>: "deceive" (in sense of cheat).

6. burst our laughing — <u>Sign</u>: "laugh" with much expression or use sign language idiom (Cup hands in front of mouth and "burst out hands" in a laughing gesture.)

7. burst out crying — <u>Sign</u>: "cry" with much expression or use sign language idiom (Dbl. "S" handshape over eyes, palms facing outward; "burst open" hands; then sign cry).

8. bring about — <u>Sign</u>: "happen through" <u>or</u> "happen because of".

9. die down, die away, die out — <u>Sign</u>: "melt", rather slowly.

10. stick to — <u>Sign</u>: "continue" <u>or</u> "stay with".

11. stick — <u>Sign</u>: "cheat".

12. lay off . . . from a job — <u>Sign</u>: "excuse" with one vigorous movement.
. . . from someone — <u>Sign</u>: "hands off" <u>or</u> "leave alone".

13. let alone — <u>Sign</u>: "leave alone".

14. wear off — <u>Sign</u>: "melt", rather slowly.

15. on the whole — <u>Sign</u>: literally <u>or</u> sign "in general".

16. to read over — <u>Sign</u>: "read" with some exaggerated casualness.

EXERCISES

Sign the following sentences, giving particular attention to the **boldface** English idioms; fingerspell all words which cannot or should not be signed.

1. The new boy was **called down** by the manager for tardiness.

2. If you make a mistake, you must **do** the work **over again**.

3. No one can help **feeling sorry for** the underdog.

4. Whatever **became of** "Baby Jane"?

5. Josephine loves to **play tricks on** Jacqueline and Geraldine!

6. The little girl **burst out crying** when her mother scolded her.

7. The ladies **burst out laughing** at the funny joke.

8. The accident **was brought about by** carelessness. (Sign "happen through")

9. The floods **were brought about by** the heavy rains. (Sign "happen because of")

10. The camp fire slowly **died away**.

11. Do you think Jacqueline will **stick to** her new job very long?

14. Jerry told Joe to **lay off**.

15. When Josephine is sick, it is best to **leave** her **alone**.

16. The effects of the drug soon began to **wear off**.

17. **On the whole**, the situation looks rather bad.

18. The boss told Jacqueline **to read over** the letters carefully.

19. Nothing ever **became of** his good intentions.

20. Little children love **to play tricks on** one another.

LESSON 14

1. **catch on** — <u>Sign</u>: "understand".

2. **beat around the bush** — <u>Sign</u>: "get off the point"; repeat several times, moving back and forth.

3. **to be taken in** — <u>Sign</u>: "fooled" <u>or</u> "deceived" in the sense of "pretend" <u>or</u> use the sign language idiom ("S" handshape on the R-hand, forearm in L-hand at elbow; Slide arm down until L-hand rests on R-wrist — it looks something like a turtle pulling its head into its shell.)

4. **cut in** — <u>Sign</u>: "cut" <u>or</u> <u>sign</u> "bother" in the sense of interrupting.

5. **off and on, so and so** — <u>Sign</u>: "5" handshape, palm down; rock it from side to side rather slowly.

6. **to be unsure of; to be uncertain of [indecision]** — <u>Sign</u>: "on the fence" by straddling two fingers of R-hand on index finger of L-hand; rock back and forth.

7. **frequent or patronize** — <u>Sign</u>: Handshapes are the same as for major or line of work; movement is a tapping of the index finger of the L-hand by the tips of the fingers of the other hand.

8. **once and for all** — <u>Sign</u>: "once and for always" <u>or</u> you could rephrase it to: "For the last time . . ."

9. **to hear of** — <u>Sign</u>: "hear about".

10. **make fun of, laugh at** — <u>Sign</u>: literally. Use sign language idiom — (Both hands with little fingers, index fingers, and thumbs out, palms facing downward; Place R-hand index finger to side of your mouth and L-hand out in front of you; move both in and out at same time 2-3 times).

11. **as a matter of fact** — <u>Sign</u>: "true" with strong expression.

12. **upside down** — <u>Mime</u> <u>Sign</u>: turning the object upside down.

13. **hard-of-hearing** — <u>Sign</u>: "H-H".

14. **to let go of** — <u>Sign</u>: "disconnect" or "disjoin". <u>Mime</u>: letting or turning something loose.

133

EXERCISES

Sign the following sentences, giving particular attention to the **boldface** English idioms; fingerspell all words which cannot or should not be signed.

1. Do you think our friend **is catching on** to this joke?

2. Jacqueline **beat around the bush** and never came to the point!

3. Josephine felt **taken in** when she found out the truth.

4. Geraldine docs not like **to be taken in by** anyone.

5. While Jerry and Josephine were dancing, John asked "May I **cut in?**"

6. Josephine detests people who are always **cutting in on** a conversation.

7. I want it understood that I'm finished with this **once and for all!**

8. Did you **hear of** Geraldine's freak accident last week?

9. I've never **heard of** that before!

10. Josephine likes **to make fun of** Geraldine sometimes.

11. Jacqueline always **laughs at** both of them.

12. **As a matter of fact**, all those figures proved to be wrong!

13. The abstract picture was hanging **upside down**, but few people noticed it.

14. Sometimes it's hard to tell whether Geraldine is deaf or **hard-of-hearing**.

15. Please **let go of** the rope, Jack!

16. The party was **so and so**.

17. He was **unsure of** the path he wanted to take.

18. I **patronize** that restaurant several times a month.

19. Some people think it is funny **to make fun of** the handicapped.

20. Bars are often **frequented** by regular customers.

LESSON 15

1. **run over . . . something** — <u>Sign</u>: "across" in sense of going over.

   . . . to the store — <u>Sign</u>: literally <u>or</u> "go over".

2. **watch out for** — <u>Sign</u>: "watch" — spell "out for".

3. **cut off . . . paper, a tree limb, meat** — <u>Mime</u>: the action indicated by showing what you are cutting and what you are cutting with.

4. **in the way** — <u>Sign</u>: literally.

5. **in vain** — <u>Sign</u>: "useless" (often the sentence must be rephrased, e.g., from: "We tried to reach him, but it was <u>in vain</u>").

6. **is the matter with** — <u>Sign</u>: "wrong with".

7. **run away . . . from home; from jail** — <u>Sign</u>: "escape".

   a "runaway horse", a "runaway car" — How would you sign these?

8. **to be well off** — <u>Sign</u>: "rich"; however, this expression does not literally mean "rich"; hence you may use sign language idiom: "money comfortable", meaning "having plenty of money".

9. **drive up to** — <u>Sign</u>: "car", but move hands forward.

10. **hand in** — <u>Sign</u>: "give" as if handing in something.

11. **named after** — <u>Sign</u>: "named for" or "named after".

12. **stand for** — <u>Sign</u>: literally or patience, bear, with emphasis.

13. **give birth to** — <u>Sign</u>: "born" or <u>Mime Sign</u>: the "act of birth".

135

EXERCISES

Sign the following sentences, giving particular attention to the **boldface** English idioms; fingerspell all words which cannot or should not be signed.

1. **Run over to** the drug store and get me a bottle of aspirin.

2. Who **ran over** Josephine's cat?

3. We have to **run over** this job again. (Sign "go over")

4. **Watch out for** speed traps when you travel by car!

5. Please **cut off** a half pound of prime roast for me.

6. The directions said to **cut out** a triangle from the folded paper.

7. Joe's arm was **cut off** in the accident!

8. The truck was **in the way** so I decided to pass it.

9. Will the war in Viet Nam be **in vain**?

10. What **is the matter with** Geraldine tonight?

11. John **ran away** from home because he was angry with his father.

12. A **runaway car** crashed into the market!

13. Jerry **drove up to** the drive-in-bank entrance.

14. The class was told to **hand in** their term papers before vacation.

15. My son was **named after** his uncle who was my closest brother.

16. Many prisoners today will not **stand for** bad treatment.

17. What do the colors on our flag **stand for**? (Sign "mean" or "show" in the sense of "represent")

18. My cow **gave birth to** a heifer last night.

19. The **runaway horse** ran across my backyard.

20. John changed jobs; he now considers himself **to be well off**.

PRACTICE TEST 5

Lessons 13 - 14 - 15

Go through this practice test without referring back to the last three lessons to see how many of the **boldface** idioms you can remember the signs for. After you have gone through the test go back over the lessons to check yourself.

1. Some boys like to **cut in** a lot at college dances.

2. The little girl **burst out crying** when her dog died.

3. This letter must be **done over**.

4. What do you think **is the matter with** our country today?

5. Please get to the point and stop **beating around the bush**!

6. We like to **patronize** stores that give good service.

7. Did you **catch on** to Harry's new joke?

8. Some people won't **stand for** any foolishness at all.

9. Why are you so **unsure of** yourself now?

10. Some people are **laid off** their jobs without warning.

11. Please don't **make fun of** my drawing; it's the best I can do.

12. Anyone who **feels sorry for** himself should be **left alone**.

13. **Drive up** to that mailbox so I can post my letter.

14. We turn the house **upside down** for spring cleaning each year.

15. My butcher will **cut off** a good piece of meat on request.

16. Please **run over** to the store for more milk.

17. Did you **hear of** the one-eyed elephant that **ran away**?

18. Were you **named after** anyone in your family?

19. **Watch out for** cars when you **cut in** on traffic.

20. Everyone wants to be **well off** in life.

21. **Hand in** your paper and I will **let you go**.

22. What **became of** your friend who used to stop by often?

Part III

Sign Language Idioms

[**Translation:** "I haven't eaten yet."]

AN INTRODUCTION TO SIGN LANGUAGE IDIOMS

American Sign Language or Ameslan contains numerous expressions that could properly be classified as "sign language idioms". These expressions are peculiar to the Language of Signs and are commonly used in informal, everyday conversation among deaf people everywhere in the country. They are idiomatic in the sense that they have definitive or particular meaning and sometimes multiple meaning in the same way that idioms in English or any other language do. These signs evolved from various origins and have been carried down by sign language users until they have become accepted "patterns of the language".

In learning to converse freely with the deaf in informal situations in general, and, more particularly with those deaf persons with minimal language skills, a working knowledge of the most frequently used sign idioms and colloquialisms is essential. This is especially true if there is to be adequate comprehension of what the deaf say and of what they are talking about at any particular time. It should be understood that many of these expressions in signs are rarely used in formal converations, i.e., in speeches, in teaching, in lecturing, or in interpreting. The more highly literate deaf person will probably tend to use less colloquialisms in his daily conversations. Much of what such person signs is in English syntax but there is always a sprinkling of idiomatic expressions whether the signer is aware of it or not because this is the natural process of conversing in sign language. Deaf lecturers, interpreters for the deaf and often teachers do make occasional use of idioms at times and in certain situations for more effective communication with their audiences. Persons performing as reverse interpreters need, without question, thorough indoctrination into colloquial sign·language and the idiomatic patterns in order to be able to reverse from signs to English. A study of sign language idioms, then, is necessary if one is to understand average, informal conversations among the deaf and to develop a useful and practical tool for efficient and effective communication with the deaf in general. However, the student should not forget that much use of gesture and facial expression is vital to colloquial expression in sign language because the slightest change gives an entirely new meaning to the idiom.

Sign language idioms rarely fit into or resemble accepted patterns of English and must be, in effect, translated to make sense in English. The student of signs should bear in mind that the language of signs is an altogether different language, completely independent of English as a language although it is possible for one to sign and fingerspell in pure English syntax. Idioms in, any given language must be interpreted according to their use and intent in that particular language.

In **Conversational Sign Language II**, the first 14 lessons of sign language idioms are presented largely by patterns for the first time, starting with the simplest, most basic patterns and advancing to the more complex ones. The last four lessons contain a mixture of idiomatic expressions which cannot be conveyed in "broken English". A graphic explanation of the handshape(s) and movement(s) needed to sign such expressions is provided instead and the student familiar with sign structure should be able to grasp most such expressions. All through Part III, English equivalents are given side by side with the idioms. The arrangement here should be of practical value not only to teachers and students, but also to linguists wishing to establish patterning of sign language structure. It should make the process of learning to use and understand colloquial signs an easier task all around and enable one to enjoy the lively and animated conversations of the deaf.

LESSON 1

THE "FINISH" IDIOM

[TRANSLATION: "Stop playing around!"]

1. **"Eat, finish, you?", "You finish eat?"** — Have you eaten yet? —or— Are you finished eating?

2. **"Finish see you?, "See finish, you?"** — Did you see that? —or— Have you seen that before?

3. **"See finish, me.", "See finish yesterday." [last night, last year, etc.]** — I've seen that before. —or— I saw that yesterday.

4. **"Bother, go away.", "Bother, finish."** — Don't bother me. —or— I can't be bothered now. —or— Stop bothering (pestering) me!

5. **"Laugh at me, finish!" (not intended to be serious or literal)** — Stop making fun of me! —or— Stop laughing at me!

6. **"Play, play, finish!"** — Stop playing (fooling) around!

7. **"Heard finish before me."** — I've already heard that —or— I've heard that one before.

8. **"Heard finish before, you?"** — Have you ever heard of that before?

9. **"Me finish!"** — I'm all through! (finished) —or— I've done that before. —or— I've completed my work.

141

10. **"Me finish!!!"** (Use both hands for "finish" — sign it vigorously.) — I'm through (with you) —or— (with that)! (This implies that you will have nothing to do with the person or thing.)

11. **"Apply finish, me."** — I've already applied (for that job).

12. **"Time finish!"** — Time is up! —or— It's time to stop now!

13. **"_____ all gone, finish!"** [Fill in blank with name of what is all gone or what you are out of.] — It's all gone! —or— There's no more left! —or— It's all sold out! —or— It's all used up now!

14. **"(He, it, etc.) gone finish!"; (zoom) (whew!)** — He's way ahead now! —or— I'm way ahead of you now!
    [Use L-index finger, pointing outward and "L" handshape on R-hand; rest R-thumb on L-index finger; move out, bringing R-thumb and finger together in a zooming action. Add "whew" only when speaking of someone else being way ahead.]

15. **"You-me race; me gone (zoom) finish!"** — If we race, I'll beat you by a long shot!

16. **"Train gone (zoom) finish, sorry!"** — Sorry, but I don't want to repeat this! —or— I forgot now what it was I said!

17. **"School finish, zoom, me!"** — When school is over, I'm going to waste no time leaving!

EXERCISES

Translate the following English sentences or ideas into sign language idioms or into approximate sign language colloquialisms. Names of persons may be spelled or you may point to another person in class as the subject of the sentence.

1. Has Jerry eaten yet?

2. Stop bothering me; I'm very busy!

3. Oh, stop making fun of me!

4. Stop fooling around and get to work!

5. I have heard that joke before.

6. We saw that wreck before.

7. Have you seen the movie, "Gone With the Wind"?

8. I'm all through with this test.

9. I'm through with you for good, period!

10. I applied for that job last month.

11. We must stop for now!

12. Sorry, but we are all out of bread now!

13. My new car is wonderful! It really has pick up power on the road!

14. If they race, Joe will beat Jerry by a long shot!

15. Sorry, but I don't have time to repeat this!

16. I saw that movie last year.

17. Sorry, but I forgot what I was saying!

18. Have you all eaten yet?

19. Did you hear that story before?

20. As soon as class is over, I'm taking out for the beach!

LESSON 2

THE "FINISH" IDIOM

[TRANSLATION: "Sorry, but I don't want to repeat this."]

1. **"Once, finish. Again not have to!"** — It's not necessary to do this more than once. —or— Once this is finished, I don't have to do it again.

2. **"Pay off (loan) yesterday, finish me."** — I paid that loan off yesterday! —or— **"Pay off new (color TV) last week, finish me."** — I paid cash for a new color TV last week.

3. **"Mail letter yesterday, finish me!"** — I mailed that letter (package, etc.) yesterday (last week, etc.)

4. **"Inform you, finish me!"** — I already told you about that! —or— You were informed by me before!

5. **"Tease me, finish you!"** — Stop teasing me! —or— Stop making fun of (poking fun at) me!

6. **"My car worn out finish!"** — My car is all beat up! —or— My car is ready for the junk heap!

7. **"Ready finish, wish me!"** — I wish I were ready for this now, but I'm not! —or— I'm not prepared for this yet, but I wish I were!

8. **"Ready test finish, wish you?"** — Don't you wish you were ready for this test?

9. **"Plan, plan, wrecked finish!"** — Our (my) plans are all fouled up now! —or— All our planning has gone down the drain!

10. **"Altogether how many (problems) finish, you?"** — How many problems have you finished altogether now?

11. **"Bawl out (him/her) finish you?"** — Have you bawled him out yet? —or— Did you bawl him out?

12. **"Finish, finish, please!"** — All right, please stop that now! —or— That's enough, please!

13. **"Money earn finish, how much you?"** — How much money have you earned so far? (To date?)

14. **"Go, go, many times, finish, me!"** — I have gone there many times. —or— I have been there many times before.

15. **"Puzzled, finish me. Whew!"** — Boy, I'm really puzzled — about that now!"

16. **"I, I, I, finish, you!"** — Stop bragging about yourself! —or— Stop being so egotistic!

EXERCISES

Translate the following English sentences or ideas into sign language idioms or into approximate sign language colloquialisms. Names of persons may be spelled or you may point to another person in class as the subject of the sentence.

1. Have you paid off the loan on your car?

2. We paid cash for our new refrigerator.

3. Did you send that package back yet?

4. I told you I mailed that letter last week!

5. Josephine told Geraldine that she had already informed her of the dance.

6. Will you please stop teasing me about the girls?

7. Jim's old car is ready for the junk pile now!

8. Don't you wish you were ready for this test?

9. I wish I were ready for that meeting!

10. All my carefully-laid plans are up in the air now!

11. Are your plans spoiled because of the rain?

12. How many problems are we supposed to finish for class tomorrow?

13. I did that before; why do I have to do it again?

14. Have you bawled your class out for not studying yesterday?

15. All right, that's enough now, please. Stop!

16. How much money have you made so far?

17. Bob has earned about $500 on his book so far.

18. Jack said he and Jenny have gone to Ocean City many times!

19. Jim didn't understand his wife's anger.

20. I wish Bob would stop bragging about himself!

LESSON 3

THE "LATE" IDIOM

1. **"Late eat, me."** — I haven't eaten yet.
   "Late eat, you?" — You haven't eaten yet?

2. **"See late, me."** — I haven't seen that yet.
   "See late movie ("_____") you?" "Late see (movie) you, late?" — You mean you haven't seen that movie ("_____") yet?

3. **"Hear late me."** — I haven't heard about that yet.
   "Hear late, you?" — You haven't heard about that yet?

4. **"Think late, me." (Sign think with emphasis.)** — I haven't thought about that/it. —or— I haven't given any thought to it yet.

5. **"Decide late, me."** — I haven't decided yet. —or— I haven't made up my mind.

   "Late decide, late you?" — You mean you haven't decided yet?
   [Another way of saying this is by straddling your left index finger with your right hand index and middle fingers and moving back and forth to indicate being "on the fence" about something.]

6. **"Late write, me late."** — I haven't written yet.
   "Late write, me. No time!" — I haven't written yet. I've had no time to do it.

7. **"Learn (_____) late, me?"** — I haven't learned this yet! —or— I haven't studied this enough yet!

8. **"Inform me, late you!"** — You haven't informed me about this yet!
   "Inform you, late me?" — You mean I haven't told (informed) you about this yet?

9. **"Give me, late, you!"** — You haven't given me any yet.

10. **"Time finish, late!"** — Time is not up yet!

11. **"Man pop up, late."** — The (service) man has not shown up yet. —or— The (service) man has not come yet.

12. **"Bawl out him, late, you!"** — You haven't bawled him out yet! —or— You didn't bawl him out yet!

13. **"Eager! Late, you!"** — You haven't shown any enthusiasm (eagerness) yet!

147

14. **"Late teach me, late, you!"** — You haven't taught me this before. —or— You didn't teach this to me yet.

15. **"Laugh at (him) late, me!"** — I didn't laugh at him! —or— I wasn't laughing at him!

EXERCISES

Translate the following English sentences or ideas into sign language idioms or into approximate sign language colloquialisms. Names of persons may be spelled or you may point to another person in class as the subject of the sentence.

1. Jane hasn't eaten yet!

2. No, I haven't seen "Gone With the Wind" yet.

3. That news is completely new to me!

4. We haven't given any thought to the matter yet.

5. I haven't made up my mind about going to Chicago yet.

6. Joe hasn't answered my letter yet.

7. I've had absolutely no time to write anything yet!

8. Jerry said he hadn't learned that yet.

9. I can't do that; I don't know how yet!

10. You mean to tell me you haven't eaten yet?

11. You mean you haven't heard about the accident?

12. You mean you haven't made up your mind yet?

13. You didn't tell me about that yet!

14. You are saying I didn't inform you? That's not true!

15. You didn't give me back my paper yet.

16. Time is not up for one more hour yet!

17. The TV man has not shown up yet.

18. I didn't see you bawl Joe out!

19. Why haven't you shown any enthusiasm in bowling yet?

20. You never taught us that before!

21. Jim was not making fun of Bob last night!

22. . The teacher hasn't shown up yet!

PRACTICE TEST 1

Lessons 1 - 2 - 3

Go through this practice test without referring back to the last three lessons to see how many of the sign language idioms or colloquialisms you can recall. After you have gone through the test, go back over the lessons to check yourself.

1. As soon as the lecture is over, we're going straight to the Rathskellar.

2. Sorry, there's no more sugar left!

3. How come you haven't made up your mind yet?

4. We haven't seen "The Godfather" yet; we plan to.

5. I forgot to mail those letters yesterday!

6. Will you please stop teasing Judy now?

7. How many algebra problems have you finished altogether now?

8. I don't think the T.V. man is here yet.

9. Betty said she hasn't written because she has had no time yet.

10. You make up your mind first, then I'll tell you about my experience.

11. I thought I told you about the meeting!

12. Jim said he has never studied physics.

13. Bob has not shown any enthusiasm for bowling lately.

14. Bill said he was sorry but he didn't care to repeat what he said.

15. If you and I race, you'll beat me easily.

16. I have already decided to go to Hawaii next year.

17. Jack has applied for a new job with the government.

18. Jim is very puzzled because Judy hasn't shown up yet.

19. How much money have you earned from your show?

20. I wish Bill would stop acting the big egotist!

21. I haven't heard a word from any of my friends yet.

22. No, we haven't eaten, thank you, but we're not really hungry.

LESSON 4

THE "THINK" IDIOM

1. **"Think easy, you?"** [Used as a challenge - as in a heated argument when one party starts to threaten the other physically; the response of the threatened person.] — So you think you're smart. Come on! [This idiom is difficult to translate but the above is appropriate.]

2. **"Think funny, you?"** — Do you think that's funny?

   [This does not mean funny in the sense of being "humorous", but rather in the sense of "ridiculing" something that is actually very serious. Expression must be rather grim.]

3. **"Think, you?"** — Do you think so?

   [Sign: "Think" with emphasis and a quizzical expression on face, letting head drop slightly. Sometimes used sarcastically.]

4. **"Think (mind)_____, you."** [Tap head twice with "think" sign; using a quizzical expression, then throw out hand and indicate "you".] — You have no sense —or— Why don't you use your head?

5. **"Think, think___?___you?"** [Sign "think" twice; then hold out hand, palm facing upward and then shrug shoulders slightly.] — What do you think about (of) it? —or— What do you think?

6. **"Think snow night, you think?"** — Do you think it will snow tonight? —or— Do you think it's going to snow tonight?

7. **"Think zero, me!"** — I can't think of anything at all. —or— I know absolutely nothing about this.

8. **"Mind frozen, me!"** [Tap head twice as in No. 4. Give an expression of momentary "shock."] — I didn't know what to think! —or— I couldn't think for a moment.

9. **"Mind stunned, me!"** [This is different from No. 8 in that the hands do not make the "freeze" sign; instead, you let your fingers drop straight down and then hold them stiffly for a while.] — I was completely dumbfounded! —or— I was so dumbstruck, I couldn't think or say anything! —or— I was so surprised that I couldn't do anything for a while.

10. **"Mind limit, me (you)!"** [Sign: "think" twice by tapping head, followed by "limit".] — I can't think of anything more right now. —or— I guess I just don't have much in the brains.

11. **"Learn, learn, can't me; mind limit!"** — I can't learn that; it's too hard for me! —or— I don't think I can learn that; I just don't have it!

12. **"Think (mind) strong, me."** — I have a strong mind or will. —or— I am not easily swayed or influenced.

13. **"Think nothing, you?" [Use quizzical expression.]** — Can't you think at all? —or— You mean you can't think of anything?

14. **"Important, think you?" [Place slight emphasis on "think".]** — Do you think it is important (worth it)? —or— Do you think it was worthwhile? —or— In your opinion, was it worth it?

15. **"Think yourself!" [Usually used in response to a question such as: "May I go with you?" or "May I join in?"]** — It's up to you. —or— Do as you please. —or— Suit yourself! —or— It all depends on you.

EXERCISES

Translate the following English sentences or ideas into sign language idioms or into approximate sign language colloquialisms. Names of persons may be spelled or you may point to another person in class as the subject of the sentence.

1. Joe thinks he's smart! I'll show him a thing or two!

2. Joe takes that very lightly; he thinks it's funny!

3. So, you think so???

4. You don't seem to have much sense!

5. Why don't you try to use your head?

6. Jean was completely dumbfounded when she learned she had won the contest.

7. Josephine was so surprised she didn't know what to think!

8. Do you really think it might snow tonight?

9. Tell me what you think about this plan.

10. Geraldine asked if she could join the girls for bowling. They said it was up to her.

11. Sometimes Jim thinks Joe is a knucklehead!

12. I can't do that; I don't know how!

13. I doubt I can learn to do that; it's too hard for me!

14. Do you think it's worthwhile going to the play?

15. I won't give in easily; I have a strong will!

16. Jack was stunned when he saw his electric bill last month.

17. I didn't expect that question so I couldn't answer it fast.

18. Jenny said she doesn't understand the instructions at all.

19. Sorry I made that mistake; guess I'm just limited!

20. If you really want to go, it's up to you!

LESSON 5

THE "ZERO" IDIOM

1. **"Funny zero."** [**The zero is made as an "O".**] — That/This/It isn't funny! —or— It's no laughing matter!

2. **"John funny zero football!"** [**The "funny zero" idiom, as used in this example, is limited to similar situations. Basically, when applied as a description for a person or action, it means that person or action is something to watch out for.**] — John is a terrific football player! —or— John is terrific in football!

3. **"Like zero!"** [**Sign: "O" with emphasis either as the letter "O" or with the "O" brought against the L palm.**] — I don't like that at all! —or— I'm not at all interested.

4. **"Respect zero, me!"** [**Sign respect, followed by a zero struck on opposite palm; add "me".**] — I have absolutely no respect for_____! —or— I don't respect_____at all!

5. **"Pity zero, me!"** [**Sign this vigorously.**] — I have absolutely no pity (sympathy) for you (him)! —or— I don't feel sorry for you at all!

6. **"Eager zero, me!"** — I'm not at all enthusiastic about this! —or— I have absolutely no enthusiasm for this!

7. **"Ambition zero, me!"** — I have no desire (wish) to do this at all! —or— I have no ambition to go on with this!

8. **"Patience zero, me!"** [**Place "O" against L palm with force.**] — I have no patience for that at all! —or— I can't tolerate that at all!

9. **"Give me zero!"** [**You imply that you feel it wasn't at all fair to you!**] — You (He, She) didn't give me any!

10. **"Feel comfortable, zero, me!"** — I was not at all comfortable! —or— I didn't feel the least bit comfortable!

11. **"Have zero, me!"** — I don't have any at all. —or— I have absolutely none!

12. **"Understand zero, me!"** — I don't understand one thing about it! —or— I can't understand this at all!

13. **"Interest zero, me!"** — I have absolutely no interest in this at all.

14. **"Money zero, me!"** — I am completely broke now! —or— I don't have any money for this!

154

15. **"Feel zero, me!"** — I didn't feel that at all. —or— I had absolutely no feeling.

16. **"Excuse zero, you!"** — You have absolutely no excuse for that.

17. **"Wrong zero!"** — There is no mistake about it! —or— There is no difference (between the two)!

EXERCISES

Translate the following English sentences or ideas into sign language idioms or into approximate sign language colloquialisms. Names of persons may be spelled or you may point to another person in class as the subject of the sentence.

1. Bob is a terrific basketball player!

2. Icy roads are certainly no laughing matter!

3. I don't like pro wrestling at all! It turns my stomach!

4. He didn't give me any at all; I didn't like it one bit!

5. He has absolutely no respect for his parents.

6. Joe has absolutely no sympathy for others at times.

7. Jane has absolutely no enthusiasm for dancing.

8. Joe can't tolerate that at all and I don't blame him!

9. I don't know why but sometimes Jack seems to have no ambition!

10. You didn't give me any pie yet!

11. Mary was very uncomfortable when Jim questioned her!

12. Sorry, I don't have any cigarettes; I quit smoking!

13. Joe doesn't have any cigarettes either.

14. Jerry said he didn't understand that speech at all!

15. Do you mean to tell me you have no interest at all in fishing?

16. Sorry I can't lend you $5.00; I have absolutely no money with me!

17. When the dentist pulled my tooth, I didn't feel anything.

18. There is simply no excuse for your behavior!

19. I made no mistakes at all on my test!

20. The twins look exactly alike; there's not one little difference between them!

LESSON 6

THE "FEEL" IDIOM

1. **"Feel deflated me."** (small, flat, cheap) [**An expression used to indicate feeling "flat" or "very small" when you have made a blunder or something you thought was correct turns out to be all wrong or just isn't so.**] — I felt so small! —or— That makes me feel about this high!

2. **"Pity you, me!"** [**Sign: "pity" or "sympathy" rather slowly but vigorously, using a sort of frowning expression.**] — I pity you! —or— You asked for it!

3. **"Heart soft, you!"** [**Tap heart area twice with open "8" handshape.**] — You are certainly (really) soft-hearted! —or— You are so sweet and kind to help me like this!

4. **"Heart zero, you!"** [**Same movement as above.**] — You have no heart at all! —or— You have absolutely no feelings!

5. **"Heart, him, whew!"** [**Sign with open "8" handshape, touch heart area gently once to show sensitivity.**] — He is very sensitive!

6. **"Heart me, whew!"** [**Same movement as above, but with emphasis.**] — I am (was) very touched! —or— I really felt for him/her!

7. **"Feel_____, me!"** — I feel hurt!

   "Feel _____, you?" — Do you feel hurt?
   [**Sign: "feel" with one brisk movement, followed by a quick shake of the hand. With emphasis added, you indicate "very hurt".**]

8. **Use open "B" handshape to make a sign as in "heart" (#6), but do not touch heart area, followed by "me" and then "you".** — You make me feel so small. (This is only approximate.) —or— What made you say that?

9. **"Feel lousy, me!"** [**In the idiomatic sense this means basically the same as feeling stupid or small as in #1 in this lesson. You feel low about some mistake in action or speech.**] — Boy, do I feel dumb about this! —or— I wish I had kept my mouth shut! —or— I feel badly about that mistake!

10. **"Feel good, me!"** [**As an idiom, this must be signed with much emphasis and expression.**] — That really made me feel good (great)!

11. **Use with the Dbl. or single open "8" handshape; move up chest quickly and briskly once with a questioning expression. [The sign is very similar to "feel" but does not mean anything connected with feelings.]** — What's up?; What's new?; What's going on?; What was that?

12. **"Feel tough, me!"** — I had the nerve to do (say) that!

157

13. **"Feel come them, feel me." [Sign: "feel" slowly with anticipatory expression.]** — I have a feeling they will come.

14. **"Feel pass, you?" [Sign as above.]** — Do you feel you will pass (this course)?

15. **"Feel about $3-$4."** — I feel it costs about three or four dollars.

16. **"Feel strong win, me!"** — I feel sure we are going to win!

EXERCISES

Translate the following English sentences or ideas into sign language idioms or into approximate sign language colloquialisms. Names of persons may be spelled or you may point to another person in class as the subject of the sentence.

1. I found myself all wrong; I felt very small!

2. I'm sorry, but you asked for it!

3. Is your teacher soft-hearted with you?

4. Sometimes it seems Bob has no heart at all!

5. Jenny is often very sensitive!

6. The surprise party for me really touched me!

7. Jim was very hurt when Jenny turned him down for a date.

8. Did you feel hurt when Jack said that?

9. What you said makes me feel so trivial!

10. I spoke too soon and I wish I'd kept my big mouth shut!

11. When Bill failed the basket, he felt very badly!

12. Jenny passed the test; she really feels great about it!

13. What's going on over there anyway?

14. Did you feel that noise? What was it?

15. Jim went up to Joe and asked him what was new.

16. I had to say that; there was no choice about it.

17. We feel that Jack and Jenny will come tonight!

18. Jerry feels he'll pass his driving test easily!

19. Joe feels a new battery will cost him about $28 or $30.

20. I have a strong feeling our team will win this game!

PRACTICE TEST 2

Lessons 4 - 5 - 6

Go through this practice test without referring back to the last three lessons to see how many of the sign language idioms or colloquialisms you can recall. After you have gone through the test, go back over the lessons to check yourself.

1. Why was Jerry so surprised to see me?

2. Jack has no patience to wait for the first bite!

3. You really seemed to be touched by what Bob said.

4. My teacher was always a soft-hearted person!

5. Bill says he thinks it may snow this weekend!

6. You have to have a strong will to stop smoking after 20 years!

7. Why do you have no respect for the police?

8. Jim says he is flat broke right now.

9. Why does Betty feel hurt?

10. Jack and Jenny both have a strong feeling they'll win at the horse races!

11. Those two cars look exactly alike: there's not one bit of difference!

12. When I look at that wreck, I don't understand how Bill came out in one piece!

13. Sometimes you have to be sensitive to the feelings of others.

14. We are all limited in some ways; not everyone can sing.

15. Do you really think this is important?

16. Why does Bill have absolutely no interest in golf?

17. Do you feel you'll pass the next test?

18. What's new in New York this weekend?

19. Judy overheard our conversation and I wish I'd kept my mouth shut!

20. When I found out I certainly didn't feel comfortable about it!

21. Sometimes Jack draws a complete blank when you ask him a question.

22. There is no excuse at all for this mess!

160

LESSON 7

THE "SUCCEED" IDIOM

[Note: In the idiomatic sense, the "succeed" sign is made with only one movement and not two as in the literal sense.]

1. **"Succeed hit me!"** — I finally made it. —or— I finally won the prize.

2. **"Succeed, finish me!"** — I finally finished the job. —or— I finally made it. —or— I finally accomplished something.

3. **"Succeed, finish, late me!"** — I haven't yet finished this!

4. **"Succeed strike (X as in bowling), me!"** — I finally made a strike! —or— Oh, boy! I got a strike at last!"

5. **"Succeed letter get, me, succeed!"** — I finally got that letter I was waiting for. —or— At last, I received a letter.

6. **"Succeed, time!"** [**With slow emphasis on "time" but with an expression of anger.**] — It's about time you got here!

7. **"Succeed late, you!"** — For once you're late!

   "Succeed on time, you!" — You finally made it on time!

8. **"Work, succeed you!"** — So you are finally working!

9. **"Laugh, succeed you!"** — You're laughing at last! —or— So I finally made you laugh!

10. **"Pop up, succeed you!"** — You finally showed up. —or— You finally made it. —or— At last you arrived.

11. **"Red face, succeed you, me!"** — I finally made you blush!

    [Sign: "red", followed by the dbl. open "B" handshape moving slowly up the sides of your face to indicate blushing.]

12. **"Imagination, succeed you!"** — You finally got your imagination to working.

13. **"Study, study, succeed you!"** — So you finally decided to study. —or— At last you made up your mind to study.

14. **"Support me, succeed you!"** — You finally came around! —or— So you're on my side for once!

15. **"Succeed fail, me."** — I finally failed to make it/one. (a strike in bowling, for example.)

EXERCISES

Translate the following English sentences or ideas into sign language idioms or into approximate sign language colloquialisms. Names of persons may be spelled or you may point to another person in class as the subject of the sentence.

1. I finally hit the jackpot!

2. I'm so happy I finally finished that boring job!

3. Joe finally got that promotion!

4. Jerry hasn't finished fixing his car yet!

5. At last, Bob has made two strikes in a row! (bowling)

6. I haven't made a strike yet!

7. Jenny is happy because she finally got that letter from Jack!

8. It's about time you finished working!

9. Jim was finally late for work today!

10. For once, Jerry and Joe were on time for the meeting!

11. Betty finally got a job with the government!

12. We finally made the girls laugh!

13. So you've finally arrived; we've waited and waited for you!

14. Bob finally made Betty blush!

15. Now you're beginning to use your imagination!

16. I'm glad you finally made up your mind to study!

17. You're finally on my side for once; it's about time!

18. I failed to hit the jackpot!

19. Jack finally failed a test for the first time in this life!

20. I finally hit on the idea after studying for a long time!

LESSON 8

THE "LIE DOWN" IDIOM

[Note: the idioms in this lesson are so classified because they all start with the sign position for "lie down".]

1. **"Lie down minute, why not you?"** — Why don't you lie down for a few minutes?

2. **"Lying (flat on back), me!"** [Make sign for "lie down"; move hand back quickly and with emphasis, sliding across opposite palm.] — I'm all worn out! —or— I'm completely exhausted now!

3. **Hold L palm open, facing upward; use the "2" handshape on R hand, palm also facing upward: lay "2" on L palm; move "2" around and around, crooking fingers off and on, followed by "me".** — I never laughed so hard in my life! —or— I was just rolling with laughter. —or— I laughed and laughed so hard! —or— I laughed until I cried. —or— It was so funny, I nearly died laughing.

4. **Use the same handshapes and positions as above; crook the "2" and move sidewise in a rocking position, striking L palm each time you come down, followed by "me" and "all night".** — I tossed and turned all night long! —or— I didn't sleep well; I had a restless night.

5. **Use the same starting position as #3 and #4, but do not place the "2" on L palm; instead, in one vigorous striking motion, bring the "2" to L palm and bounce up immediately. [Varying degrees of emphasis and expression will convey different meanings.] [May be signed with R palm facing L palm.] [May add the "phooey" sign.]** — We lost! —or— Our team lost! —or— We lost again, phooey!

6. **Use above position with the "2" resting palm down on the L palm; turn over the "2" quickly. Add "me". [This position and movement are also used in expressions like: "He'll turn over in his grave!"]** — I flipped! I just couldn't believe it!

7. **Starting with the "2" in L hand, right palm facing upward, lift R hand slowly, crooking the "2" off and on rapidly; let R hand fall back to L palm. Follow with "me" and the "whew!" sign.** — I just about hit the ceiling when I heard that. —or— I just about jumped out of my skin!

8. **Using the same movement but changing to a standing position, gives the idea of extreme elation.** — I'm jumping up and down with joy!

9. **Start with a lying position as above; move rapidly to a rigid standing position, followed by "me".** — Boy! Did I jump out of bed! —or— I was so startled, I jumped out of bed immediately.

10. **"Lie down quiet, me, dreaming." [Sign "quiet" and "dream" very slowly with emphasis.]** — I was just lying very quietly letting my mind wander.

11. **"Lie down, can't me!"** — I just can't seem to lie still long enough to rest. —or— I just can't seem to rest.

12. **Place the "2" in L palm: move both hands forward in 2 or 3 revolutions. Indicate subject by name or referent.** — (Who?) has been bedridden for (How long?) now. —or— (Who?) has been unable to get up and around.

EXERCISES

Translate the following English sentences or ideas into sign language idioms or into approximate sign language colloquialisms. Names of persons may be spelled or you may point to another person in class as the subject of the sentence.

1. When I finished that job, I was worn out!

2. His joke was so funny, we all nearly died laughing!

3. Bob was completely exhausted after house painting all day.

4. Geraldine laughed until she cried when she heard that story!

5. Everybody was just rolling with laughter at the play Saturday night!

6. Joe tossed and turned all night long because he was worried.

7. You look like you had a restless night!

8. Our boys lost another game!

9. Jim flipped when he saw the grocery bill!

10. I just about jumped through the ceiling when my wife woke me!

11. The girls are jumping with joy because our boys finally won!

12. The noise startled Jenny so much, she jumped right out of bed!

13. I like to lie down from time to time and just let my mind wander.

14. I can't seem to lie still; I just toss and turn!

15. Grandma was bedridden seven years before she died.

16. Governor Wallace was in the hospital a long time after he was shot.

17. When I broke my heel, I couldn't get around for a while.

18. The slightest vibration can make a very tired person practically jump out of his skin!

19. Why did you jump like that when I woke you?

20. Joe discovered he had overslept and, boy, did he jump out of bed!

LESSON 9

THE "FOR-FOR" IDIOM

[NOTE: "Why" may be substituted for the "for-for" in most examples here.]

1. **"For-for?"** [**Add an object by pointing to something.**] — What for? —or— Why? ——What's that here for? —or— Why is that here?

2. **"Talk, talk, for-for?"** — What are you talking (so much) for? —or— Why are you talking about that? (It's supposed to be kept quiet!)

   [**May substitute "do" in the sense of action, "argue", or other such words for "talk".**] — Why are you doing that? —or— What are you arguing for?

3. **"Laugh at me, for-for?"** — What are you laughing so hard for? —or— What's so (darn) funny?

   [**May switch to another object or person in place of "me".**] — What are you making fun of (Joe) for?

4. **"Work, work, for-for?"** [**May substitute "play" or "study" or other such words for "work".**] — What are you working so hard for? —or— Why are you working like that?

5. **"Red faced, for-for?"** — What are you embarrassed about? —or— Why are you so embarrassed?

   If "embarrassed" is substituted for "red-faced" and signed slowly, it would mean: Why are you so shy?

6. **"Blame, blame, me, why (for-for)?"** — Why are you blaming me? —or— Why are you trying to find fault with me?

7. **"Face expression, for-for (why)?"** — Why are you making faces? —or— What's the idea of making faces (at me)?

8. **"Eager, you, for-for?"** [**Sign: "eager" with vigor.**] — What are you so enthusiastic/anxious about? —or— Why are you so eager/anxious?

9. **"Hungry, hungry, for-for?"** [**Here "hungry" is signed in rapid succession two or three times, referring to sexual hunger or passion. It is more often used in jest or teasing than it is in seriousness.**] — What are you passionate for? —or— Why are you so passionate?

10. **"Worry, worry, for-for?"** — What are you so worried about? —or— Why are you so worried?

11. **"Money, money, for-for?"** — What do you need money for? —or— Why do you need money?

12. **"Go, for-for?" [Why go, why?]** — What should I go (there) for? —or— Why should I bother going?

13. **"Imagination you, for-for (why)?"** — Why are you imagining things? —or— What are you letting your imagination work overtime for?

14. **"Funny! For-for (why)?" [Sign: "funny" very slowly and with a half-suspicious look]** — I have a feeling there's something funny going on and I wonder what. —or— That's strange! I wonder what (John did that for)?

15. **"Foolish, foolish, for-for?" [Use the Dbl. "Y" handshape; move both hands alternately in front of forehead.]** — What are you fooling (playing) around for? —or— Why are you behaving in a foolish way?

16. **"Stay up all night, for-for?"** — Why did you stay up all night? —or— What did you stay up all night for?

EXERCISES

Translate the following English sentences or ideas into sign language idioms or into approximate sign language colloquialisms. Names of persons may be spelled or you may point to another person in class as the subject of the sentence.

1. Why was John making funny faces at the meeting?

2. Why are you blaming Jerry for that?

3. What's the use of studying hard if you can't get anything out of it?

4. Why work hard on such a lovely day?

5. What was the reason for that noise?

6. What are you fooling around here for?

7. If you didn't like it, why did you bother going in the first place?

8. Why were the Hansens up all night?

9. What's that thing for?

10. What did you talk so much for?

11. Why are you so worried about the time?

12. Why is Jerry imagining things now?

13. What does Judy need the money for now? She's borrowed enough!

14. Why are you so anxious to leave work early today?

15. What was Jenny blushing for a while ago?

16. Why are the boys laughing at Joe?

17. Why should we go there if we don't want to?

18. I thought it odd John never showed up! I wonder why!

19. Why are you erasing the boards? I thought the teacher said to leave the lesson on.

20. What are you so moody for? Cheer up!

PRACTICE TEST 3

Lessons 7 - 8 - 9

Go through this practice test without referring back to the last three lessons to see how many of the sign language idioms or colloquialisms you can recall. After you have gone through the test, go back' over the lessons to check yourself.

1. Have you finally been able to get a job?

2. What are you working so hard for?

3. Bill and Betty really cracked up over that joke!

4. Did you have a restless night because of the heat, too?

5. You should have seen Jenny; was she shy!

6. I haven't succeeded in finishing this paper yet!

7. You'd be completely exhausted, too, if you had to carry sand all day!

8. Why is Bob standing over there frowning?

9. What did Betty stay up all night for?

10. If you won the state lottery, you'd be jumping with joy, too!

11. I see you finally got your imagination working again!

12. Why are Bob and Betty making fun of Judy?

13. I wish you wouldn't talk so much!

14. How long will you be bedridden after your operation?

15. Why are you blaming Jim for your own mistake?

16. What do you need money for?

17. Jenny finally got the letter she was waiting for.

18. Well, I'm glad you finally showed up!

19. Have you any idea why Bob and Betty are fooling around?

20. I don't think we will lose this game.

21. Be glad Jack and Jenny finally made it on time for once!

22. Maybe next time I'll succeed in making a few strikes (bowling).

LESSON 10

THE DEROGATORY IDIOMS

1. **"Stink you!"** (me, him, etc.) [**Hold thumb and index finger over nose; shake head rather vigorously; point to "you" or to self.**] — You were lousy! —or— You did (played) terribly! —or— I was lousy (I did very, very poorly!).

2. **"Selfish, you!"** (me) [**Sign "selfish" with emphasis.**] — You are very selfish! (stingy —or— You think only of yourself!

3. **"Hypocrite, you!"** [**Put R hand on L hand, palms facing downward; push left fingers down under strongly once.**] — You are two-faced! —or— You are a big hypocrite!

   "Hypocrite, who?" — Who's a hypocrite? —or— Who is being two-faced?

4. **"Fault (blame) yourself!"** [**Substitute myself or himself for "myself".**] — It's all your own fault! —or— You asked for it! —or— Blame yourself! —or— You've nobody to blame but yourself! —or— Well, I guess it's all my fault!

5. **"Vomit, me!"** [**This may look a rather vulgar sign, but it is commonly used to indicate intense repulsiveness to something.**] — I hate that! —or— I can't stand that! (stomach that)

6. **"Me sick that!"** — I'm sick of that —or— I hate that! —or— That makes me sick!

7. **"Stomach turnover, me!"** — That makes me sick to my stomach. —or— That turns my stomach! —or— I can't stomach that!

8. **"Disgusted, me!"** — I am totally disgusted with that! —or— I feel nauseated when I think of that!

   [**With a slow, determined movement, meaning is DIFFERENT. Use the same sign as above, but move more gently; use a half-smile expression; then sign "me" or "you"**] — I feel so stupid about that! —or— I never thought of it that way before! —or— I should have thought of that myself!

9. **"Me sick, you!"** [**Here "sick" is made with the "open-8" handshape as usual, but instead of just bringing the middle finger to the forehead, touch the forehead sidewise and move finger and hand in a small semi-circle with emphasis.**] — I am sick and tired of your ways! —or— I detest you! (I hate your behavior) —or— I don't like your attitude at all!

10. **"I, I, I, you!"** [**Don't sign "I" as a personal pronoun; instead burst "I's" up, striking against the chest. "You" can be replaced by "him", "her" and in the case of "self-jesting", even "me".**] — You are a big egotist! —or— You think only of yourself! —or— You are a big braggart! —or— You like to think only of yourself!

11. "Stupid, you! (me, him, etc.)'" — You are very stupid!

    [With a slow movement, meaning is DIFFERENT.] "Stupid, me!" — I don't know the answer to that! —or— I don't know how to do this!

12. "Nervy (bold) (fresh), you!" — You have some nerve! —or— You are very bold (forward/fresh)! —or— The nerve of you!

13. "Tough, him (you, me, etc.)!'" — Boy, is he tough! —or— He is really hard-hearted! —or— He is brash!

14. "Strict, you! Whew!" [May be used seriously or in fun.] — You certainly are very strict!

15. "Famous late you, famous!" [Sign: "famous" with only one vigorous movement instead of the usual two.] — You are always late! —or— You are famous for being late!

16. "Red face, you!" (me) [Don't sign "face" in the sense of "look"; rather, use a Dbl. "curved-L" handshape to indicate a "round, blushing face"] — Your face is as red as a beet!

17. "Embarrassed, me!" [Don't sign "embarrass" in the usual way, but, using the Dbl. "5" handshape, palms facing in, bring hands sharply and quickly up over face in one strong movement; add "me".] — I was extremely embarrassed! —or— His behavior embarrassed me terribly. —or— I was never so embarrassed in my whole life!

18. "Imagination, too much, you!" — Your imagination is working overtime! —or— You are imagining too much!

    "Imagination, stop (finish)" — Stop imagining so much! —or— Stop letting your imagination run wild! —or— Stop speculating so much!

    "Imagination, you (me, him)!" [Use the Dbl. "I" handshape, but repeat several times rapidly; add "you", "me", "him".] — You are imagining things! —or— You are letting your imagination run away with you.

19. "Look up and down at you, me!" [Often used in response to some misdeed or stupid act of one kind or another; sometimes used in jest or teasing.] — I wonder about you! —or— Well, just look at you now! —or— Aren't you the stupid one now!

171

EXERCISES

Translate the following English sentences or ideas into sign language idioms or into approximate sign language colloquialisms. Names of persons may be spelled or you may point to another person in class as the subject of the sentence.

1. I hate petty gossip!

2. John is really heartless! He has very little sympathy!

3. When you saw the accident, did it turn your stomach?

4. That man has some nerve asking me for a date!

5. I'm sick and tired of this changing weather!

6. I really don't know how to do this!

7. You looked like you were never so embarrassed in your life!

8. Oh, stop letting your imagination run wild!

9. Why are you always late?

10. You are letting your imagination run away with you!

11. Joe likes to think only of himself. He is one big egotist!

12. Jerry played a very poor game last night!

13. You are being very selfish!

14. I felt cheap when I found out how wrong I was!

15. I don't like your attitude at all!

16. The whole matter was disgusting to me!

17. Some people are sometimes two-faced!

18. I have no one to blame for that except myself!

19. You have no one to blame for this trouble except yourself!

20. When Jerry dropped his tray of food, Joe gave him a look from head to toe!

21. Who did you say was a two-faced friend?

22. Mr. Hardenhead is really a very strict teacher!

23. The whole idea is so repulsive to me!

24. I feel so stupid for not thinking about that myself!

25. Jerry's face was as red as a beet!

LESSON 11

MIXED IDIOM PATTERNS

I. The "Worthless/Useless" Pattern:

1. **Bring Dbl. "9" handshape together like in "worth"; move out in opposite directions, quickly opening to a Dbl. "5" handshape. [Give an expression of "dismay" or "hopelessness".]** — It's no use at all! —or— It looks completely hopeless!

2. **Use the same idiom as above; add "argue".** — It's no use arguing! —or— Arguing will do you no good! —or— Arguing will not help one bit! —or— You will get nowhere by arguing!

3. **Use the same idiom as above; add "study".** — It's no use studying this. —or— What good will it do to study this?

4. **Precede the "worthless", or "worth nothing" idiom with the sign for "upset, me!" Follow with "eat". [May reverse order and substitute "sleep", "study", etc. for "eat".]** — I'm too upset to eat now! —or— It's no use eating; I'm just too upset!

5. **Precede the "worthless" idiom with "go".** — It won't help to go. —or— It's too late to go.

6. **Precede the "worthless" idiom with the sign for "bawl out"; follow with "him", etc.** — It's no use bawling him out; he won't learn from it! —or— Save your breath! It won't do any good to bawl him out!

7. **Precede the "worthless" idiom with "talk, talk, talk, they", followed by the sign for "cut in".** — They just kept on talking; it was useless trying to get a word in.

II. The "Why Not" Pattern:

1. **"Why not teach me, why not you?"** — Why don't you teach me how to do this?

2. **"Play, why not, you?"** — Why don't you get out and play? —or— You ought to get out and exercise; don't you know that?

3. **"Support me, why not, you?"** — Why didn't you stand up for (support) me?

III. The "Won't Me" Pattern:

1. **"Help, won't me!" [Emphasize "won't".]** — I absolutely refuse to give any help!

2. **"Forgive, won't me!" [Emphasize "won't".]** — I will never forgive (him for that)!

174

IV. The "Will You" Pattern:

1. **"Lose, will you!"** [**Place emphasis on initial word.**] — You will lose for sure! —or— It's a gamble! You're likely to lose! —or— The odds are against you!

2. **"Sorry, will you!"** [**Place emphasis on initial word.**] — You will be very sorry (if you go ahead with that)!

3. **"Sick, will you!"** [**Place emphasis on initial word.**] — You will be sick for sure (if you eat that)! —or— You will really become sick (if you go there)!

4. **"Mad, will you?" Change emphasis to "will you?" but on a "soft tone".** — Will you get mad (at me) (if I do that)?

EXERCISES

Translate the following English sentences or ideas into sign language idioms or into approximate sign language colloquialisms. Names of persons may be spelled or you may point to another person in class as the subject of the sentence.

1. The whole thing looks completely hopeless!

2. I told Joe that arguing would do him no good!

3. I want to learn bowling; why don't you teach me?

4. It's no use studying tonight; it's too hot!

5. It was no use eating; we were too upset after the accident.

6. Why don't you go out and play a game of volleyball?

7. Don't waste energy! It won't help one bit to bawl him out for that; he just won't learn!

8. I can't sleep now; I'm too upset about this!

9. It's no use going to the movies now; we're too late!

10. Why didn't you get up and support me at the meeting?

11. After what happened, I simply refuse to help that group!

12. Betty said she would never forgive Bob now!

13. If you bet again, you're likely to lose your last dollar!

14. You'll be very sorry if you don't come to my party!

15. If you eat any more green apples, you'll be sick for sure!

16. I'll get mad if you don't stop teasing me!

17. Why not ask for a date with Jenny if you like her so much?

18. Bill won't go with Jack to the lake.

19. The odds are against you in this race! (horses)

20. It won't help to talk now; it's all over!

MIXED IDIOM PATTERNS

[TRANSLATION: "You look just like your father!"]

I. The "Hungry/Wish" Pattern:

[NOTE: "Hungry" is signed with the "C" handshape, fingers and thumb touching chest below throat; move down body to stomach level. For "wish", stop at chest level just above stomach area.]

1. **"Hungry, me!"** — I am hungry.

   [With added emphasis, "hungry" becomes "starved"] — I am starved! —or— I'm starving!

2. **"Hungry, you?"** — Are you hungry?

3. **"Go, wish, you?"** — Don't you wish you could go too? —or— Do you really want to go along? [See other examples in #15 and #16 in Lesson 18.]

II. The "Whew" Pattern:

1. **"Beautiful, whew!"** [Indicate the what or whom you are referring to as "very beautiful". Sign "beautiful" slowly and with emphasis.] — It was just beautiful! —or— It was the most beautiful thing! —or— I never saw any place quite so beautiful!

2. **"Awful, whew!"** [Use appropriate expression; a "sour look" or "frown".] — It was simply awful! —or— I thought it was rather disgusting!

3. **"Funny you, whew!"** [Use a laughing expression; <u>sign</u> funny slowly and with emphasis] — You were so funny! —or— I thought you were so comical!

4. **"Look strong father, you! Whew! Wrong, zero!"** [Emphasize the sign for "strong".] — You look just like your father! There is no difference between the two of you. —or— You are an exact copy of your father!

5. **"Eager, me, whew!"** [Rub palms back and forth together briskly to indicate degree of enthusiasm.] — I'm really enthusiastic about it. —or— I'm anxious to see what comes of it. —or— I'm really very much interested in this!

6. **"Interest me, whew!"** [May substitute "like" or any other similar word for interest. Place emphasis on the sign, "interest".] — I am very interested in that. —or— I like that very much.

III. The "Money" Pattern:

1. **"Money comfortable, you!"** [Put emphasis on the sign for "comfortable".] — You are well off! —or— You are well-to-do!

2. **"Money much (or lots), they."** [Add emphasis on "money much" to mean very rich.] — They are rich! —or— They have lots of money!

3. **"Money, many?"** [Here <u>sign</u> "many" with one hand and just one movement upward.] — How much money does this cost? —or— What's the price?

4. **"Money earn, many, guess, you!"** — (You) Guess how much money I make (earn)?

5. **"Altogether, how much worth (money), figure you?"** — How much do you think (feel) (it) will cost altogether?

IV. The "Questioning" Pattern:

1. **"Funny!"** [Use a serious expression, indicating puzzlement and emphasize the sign "funny" with one slow movement.] — I don't understand that! —or— I thought that was strange! —or— That is puzzling, really!

2. **"Strange (odd), true!"** [<u>Sign</u> as directed in #1 above.] — That's really strange! —or— I think that's certainly odd!

EXERCISES

Translate the following English sentences or ideas into sign language idioms or into approximate sign language colloquialisms. Names of persons may be spelled or you may point to another person in class as the subject of the sentence.

1. Are you very hungry now?

2. Jean and I are simply famished! Where's the food?

3. I'm very much interested in bridge!

4. You look just like your sister! Are you twins?

5. The Browns are very well-to-do people!

6. Jacqueline thought her husband was rich before she married him.

7. John is really enthusiastic about his new job.

8. I really wish I could go with you, but I'm so busy right now!

9. Can you estimate how many people were there last night?

10. How much money do you need?

11. The mountains were simply beautiful!

12. That girl is indescribably beautiful!

13. The play was simply awful in my opinion!

14. Jerry is so funny at times!

15. I thought that was very strange!

16. Joe thought that was very odd, too!

17. Jerry likes to be funny sometimes!

18. Do you want to join us for dinner?

19. How much money do you have for tonight?

20. Can you guess how much money Jack and Jenny will make together?

Lessons 10 - 11 - 12

Go through this practice test without referring to the last three lessons to see how many of the sign language idioms or colloquialisms you can recall. After you have gone through the test, go back over the lessons to check yourself.

1. I thought we played a lousy game last night!

2. It's no use arguing with Betty when she is mad!

3. The Grand Canyon is a beautiful, breathtaking sight, they say!

4. Why didn't you teach Jack how to bowl?

5. You'll be sorry if you don't go to the dance!

6. Everyone wishes to be rich at times.

7. The sight of that crushed cat made my stomach turn!

8. Bob says he doesn't know anything about astrology.

9. Why did you say you won't help?

10. The floods around here from Agnes were simply awful!

11. How much does that T.V. cost?

12. You'll get mad if I tell you the truth!

13. We had to look at Bill and wonder after his clumsy mistake!

14. You should stop imagining things; it won't help you at all.

15. Are Bob and Betty very hungry now?

16. I wish you'd get up in the meetings and support me sometimes!

17. Why is Joe's face so red?

18. Bill thought Bob had a lot of nerve taking his beer!

19. I wish I'd thought of that myself!

20. Jack has no one to blame but himself, really!

21. You are right! I am selfish!

22. It won't do any good to ask Bill for money; he doesn't have any.

LESSON 13

MIXED IDIOM PATTERNS

I. The "You???" Pattern:

[NOTE: In this pattern, one is always expressing wonderment or amazement at the other person's tastes or attitudes. The emphasis must be on "you" accompanied by a facial expression indicative of puzzlement.]

1. **"Eager, you??"** — Are you really enthusiastic about this?

2. **"Like, you??"** [**Give the impression that you don't like it.**] — Do you really like that?

3. **"Busy, you??"** — Are you really busy?

   [**If done in a sarcastic manner, add sign for "phooey!" which is made by holding hand up and brushing it down through the air.**] — You call that being busy?

4. **"Worry, you?? Phooey!"** — What are you worried (worrying) about?

5. **"Think you?? Phooey!"** — You are silly to think that way!

6. **"Laugh you?? Phooey!"** — You are silly to laugh at that (or me)! —or— I'll have the last laugh yet!

II. More Simple "ME" Patterns:

1. **"Sorry, me!"** — I'm very, very sorry about that!
   [**Sign "sorry" very slowly.**] — I'm very sorry for you!

2. **"Sorry, me!"** [**Sign "sorry" slow, emphatic movement.**] — That's just too bad!

3. **"Worry, me, whew!"** [**"Whew" here is not in the usual sense because it is related to a serious problem; therefore, shake your hand once with a hard movement.**] — I'm so worried about this now! —or— I am just sick with worry about this!

4. **"Worry, me? Phooey!"** — Do you think I'm worried about that? Heck no!

5. **"Angry, me!"** [**Use the "angry" sign in the sense of being mad enough to pull off your shirt and start fighting — use both hands in the "crooked-5" handshape as if grasping your shirt tails and move hands up miming the removal of your shirt.**] — I was so mad about that! —or— I was never so angry (mad) in my whole life!

6. **"Not like, me!"** — I didn't like it (that) one iota (bit)!

181

7. **"Tired out, me!"** [**Sign "tired" somewhat like "admitting", but instead of bringing hands up as in "admit" or "confess", drop hands out and down with first a slow and then a quickening motion.**] — I'm all in now! —or— I'm complately exhausted! —or— I'm simply pooped!

8. **"Resist, me!"** [**Sign "resist" as in "guard" or "defend", but with only one hand and a strong facial expression indicative of resistance.**] — I put up a good resistance to (that)! —or— I refused to be tempted at all!

III. A "Mimic" Idiom Pattern:

1. **"Cut it!"** [**Pantomime clipping a pair of scissors in front of your mouth.**] — Stop talking right now! —or— That's enough talking for now!

2. **Mime Sign clipping a pair of scissors in front of yourself.** — That's enough for now! —or— O. K. it's time to stop that now!

EXERCISES

Translate the following English sentences or ideas into sign language idioms or into appropriate sign language colloquialisms. Names of persons may be spelled or you may point to another person in class as the subject of the sentence.

1. John, are you very busy right now?

2. You think you're busy??

3. Do you really like yogurt?

4. Jean was never so mad in her life!

5. I didn't like that one bit!

6. I'm very, very sorry about that!

7. O.K., stop talking now!

8. Is Jim really very interested in boxing?

9. You think Joe is worried? Forget it!

10. Jerry is so worried about his girlfriend!

11. Jenny refuses to be influenced by those girls!

12. Bob and I are completely exhausted after that long hike in the mountains!

13. Can Jim resist a pretty girl like Jeannie? I don't think he can!

14. Does Joey really like turnip greens?

15. Why are you so worried? There's nothing to worry about now!

16. You are being foolish to think like that!

17. So you think that's funny? Just wait and see!

18. I'm very sorry about your problem!

19. It's just too bad you won't listen to us!

20. Why was Betty so hopping mad the other day?

LESSON 14

MIXED IDIOM PATTERNS

I. More Simple "ME" Patterns:

1. **"Disbelieve, me!"** [<u>Sign</u> "doubt" using the "crooked-2" handshape placed in front of your eyes and nose; pull fingers forward crooking them twice as you move out; add "me".] — I doubt that very much —or— I don't think so.

2. **"Disbelieve, me!"** [Use the same sign and movement as above but move out only once very forcefully.] — I don't believe it at all!

3. **"Support me, you?"** [If asking for full support, simply increase emphasis on the sign "support".] — Will you stand up for me? —or— Will you give me your support?

4. **"Heard never before, me!"** — I've never heard of that before! —or— I've never heard of such a thing before.

II. Varied Compound Patterns:

1. **"Look at me, stop, not nice!"** [Repeat "look at" a few times.] [The "finish" sign may be used in place of "stop".] — Stop looking at me like that; you embarrass me!

2. **"Pop up, not expect!"** [Indicate who or what popped up.] — He showed up unexpectedly! —or— The Smiths unexpectedly dropped in.

3. **"Get even him, hungry (wish) me!"** [Sign "get even with" by using the "open-B" handshape, palms down and L hand out in front of R hand; bring fingers sharply together, bouncing fashion, and separate again.] — I'd just like to get even with him! —or— I just wish I could show him!

III. Repeating Patterns:

1. **"Foolish, foolish, foolish, me!"** [Here, move the Dbl. "Y" handshapes alternately in circles in front of forehead accompanied by a smiling expression.] — I was just playing around having fun! —or— I was just fooling around for the fun of it!

2. **"Me bawl out, bawl out him!"** [Use the Dbl. "S" handshape, one "S" on top of the other; place both up at forehead; move out vigorously and repeatedly into a Dbl. "5" handshape.] — I bawled him out good! —or— I simply blasted him!

   [Reverse movement towards self and add "he" or "she".] — I was bawled out by him! —or— He blasted me!

184

3. **"Struggle, struggle fix, fail, me!"** [For "struggle", use the Dbl. "1" handshape, L hand in front of R; move in small circular movements.] Indicate what you tried to fix.] — I tried and tried to fix (this) but I failed (or I couldn't do it.)!

4. **"Struggle, struggle — succeed fix, finish me!"** [Any problem requiring some effort to solve may be substituted for "fix".] — I worked and worked and finally I succeeded in fixing (this).

5. **"Blame, blame me, always, they!"** — They are always blaming me for something! —or— They are always accusing me of something! —or— They are always finding fault with me!

6. **"Hard, hard, hard, hard; not easy!"** [Repetition of "hard" is done at a medium pace and rather gently.] — It will be very difficult to do this. —or— This is hard to do; it won't be easy at all.

7. **"Earn, earn, earn, me!"** [Repetition of "earn" here is rather rapid and with a sweeping upward movement.] — I'm trying to get all I can out of this! —or— I don't miss one chance to get all I can from this!

8. **"Work, work, work, me!"** [Often used in gaining sympathy in the attempt to get others to "feel sorry for you".] — I've been working so hard lately!

   [May also mean that you worked so hard to no avail.] — I worked so hard for nothing!

Translate the following English sentences or ideas into sign language idioms or into appropriate sign language colloquialisms. Names of persons may be spelled or you may point to another person in class as the subject of the sentence.

1. I don't believe a word you say!

2. We doubt very much that we will go!

3. It seems I have worked so hard for nothing!

4. Poor Jerry has been so overworked lately!

5. I'm asking you for your full support now!

6. Don't look at me like that; you embarrass me!

7. My friends unexpectedly dropped by for a surprise visit!

8. Do you like friends to drop in on you unexpectedly?

9. John said he never heard of that before!

10. What are you bawling me out for?

11. Are you trying to find fault with me?

12. You shouldn't try to get even if someone does wrong to you.

13. I don't think that can be done very easily!

14. Do you like to get all you can out of something?

15. Joey was just fooling around when he found the silver dollar!

16. Bob tried and tried to get the starter working but he failed!

17. After working hard for four hours, Joe finally succeeded in fixing the stopped-up toilet!

18. We worked and worked half the night to find the answers to these problems! (math)

19. Betty said she had never heard of that story before.

20. I just don't believe it will snow tonight!

LESSON 15

MISCELLANEOUS IDIOMS

[TRANSLATION: "I flattered my teacher"]

[NOTE: In this lesson, and the ones following, are grouped those sign language idioms which cannot be expressed even in broken English and which do not fall into any particular pattern. Their structure and movement must be explained carefully. Their translations are more or less approximate.]

1. Use "open-C" handshape toward chest with fingers on chest; grasp slowly to a close ("S") as you bring hand(s) downward; add "me", "you", "him" etc. [This sign implies "holding back an outburst of emotional anger, usually a response to someone's open provocation of your intentions or those of another person, if you are talking about his reactions.] [Use of both hands with a more vigorous movement adds emphasis.] — I had to control myself. —or— He had a hard time controlling his temper. —or— (You) Restrain (control) yourself!

2. Use the Dbl. "1" handshape, fingers pointing outward like a gun, L hand slightly ahead of the R; jab fingers forward briskly once; indicate what you despise or hate. — I hate that person! —or— I despise that with all my heart! —or— I simply can't stand the idea.

3. Use "S" handshape, forearm in L hand at elbow; slide arm down until L hand rests on right wrist; add "me". — Boy, I really felt like pulling my head in! —or— I certainly felt like an idiot!

4. Use "C" handshape in front of nose [single or double]; draw out to an "S" handshape vigorously; add "me". — That held my interest —or— That drew my attention (Indicate the direction or attention) —or— I was strongly attracted by/to that.

187

5. Use "open-C" handshape, fingers touching throat; bring to a closed "S" at the base of the throat; follow by "me" or "you". [This sign implies holding back an outburst of laughter" when someone says or pulls a "boner".] — I could hardly hold back my laughter! —or— It was hard for me to keep from saying anything.

6. Use the Dbl.-"F" handshape, palms facing each other; strike left "F" with the right (Use appropriate expression). — That's not fair! —or— That's not right! (in the sense of being fair)

   Add "you" for this Translation: You're not being fair to me! —or— You're not treating me right!

7. Use "1" handshape on L hand; brush the "1" with your R hand several times slowly; add "you", "him" or "me". — You are an apple-polisher —or— You are buttering up_____!

8. Use the Dbl.-"1" handshape and position pointing outward like a gun; move fingers alternately out and back. Add "you", etc. [To give impression of "very insulting", simply increase emphasis on the sign.] — He's very insulting! —or— I taunted (teased) him about his behavior.

9. Use the Dbl.-"1" handshape to represent your legs, pointing fingers out and slightly down; let both come over backwards; then sign "me". — I was completely flabbergasted! —or— I literally fell over (when I heard that).

10. Use the Dbl.-"5" handshape; palms in front of your face; breeze both hands past your face; add "me". — I have complete freedom to go ahead with this. —or— I have authority to go ahead with this! —or— I have a right to do this!

11. Use the single-"1" handshape in front of the forehead; move back to head as in making a question mark; add "me" (Expression should show extreme puzzlement). — I was extremely puzzled! —or— I don't understand that at all!

12. Use Dbl. handshape of index fingers and little fingers pointed outward, palms facing downward; place right index finger at right side of mouth, holding L hand out slightly; move both hands out a short distance and back simultaneously 2 or 3 times. — [Equivalent to: "Ha! Ha! Ha!" —or— to the idea that you don't take the other person seriously in what he says or is doing. Also, used in making fun of another person having to work hard when you are free to loaf or do nothing.]

13. Use the Dbl.-"B" handshape with L palm facing right; place the right "open-B" handshape on top of the L hand. Move up in jerky, wiggling movements and back. [Varying degrees of emphasis will indicate amount of anger.] — boy! I really blew my lid! (Top) —or— I raised the devil about that!

14. Use "1" handshape on R hand, hold out slightly, palm facing outward; place back tip of right index finger at nose, move it down to L palm rather vigorously sliding forward briefly; add "me". [Used to indicate falling for material things or something beautiful.] — I fell in love with it! —or— It was love at first sight!

    [Precede sign with "me"; follow it with "her" or "him".] — I fell in love with her at first sight!

15. Make handshape with thumb, index finger, and little finger out; hold hand upright towards the person that you love or for whom you wish to profess love. [May be translated loosely or literally.] — I.L.Y. —or— I love you!!!!!

    [May be used as an expression of "love" for another person's good deed toward you or for you.] — I love you for that, you big sweet thing!

16. Use the "B" handshape on the R hand and the "5" handshape on the L, palm facing you; position R hand near the left thumb and move past the whole L hand. [This presents sequence from the beginning to the end.] — It (the book) (the movie) was good from the beginning to the end.

EXERCISES

Translate the following English sentences or ideas into sign language idioms or into approximate sign language colloquialisms. Names of persons may be spelled or you may point to another person in class as the subject of the sentence.

1. Oh, goodie! I can go to the beach while you have to study!

2. You're not fair at all!

3. That movie held my attention from the beginning to the end!

4. I was so mad about that, but I held my anger back.

5. When Joe said that, I had to hold back an outburst of laughter!

6. I could hardly keep from laughing out loud!

7. I think Bob is being unfair to all of us!

8. I was completely flabbergasted when I found I had won the prize!

9. Joe likes to "butter up" his boss!

10. Jerry thinks he has a right to do as he pleases!

11. Jerry fell in love with Josephine at first sight!

12. I love you for that; I could kiss you!

13. I fell for that cute little dog the first time I saw her!

14. I detest people who butt in on a conversation!

15. We teased Jim about his new girl friend.

16. Jerry really blew his top when he learned that Joe was going with Judy!

17. My father used to raise the devil when we came home late!

18. Jim felt like hiding when I beat him; he thought I couldn't do it!

19. Josephine was extremely puzzled over that letter!

20. We had to fight to hold back the tears during the last part of that movie!

PRACTICE TEST 5

Lessons 13 - 14 - 15

Go through this practice test without referring to the last three lessons to see how many of the sign language idioms or colloquialisms you can recall. After you have gone through the test, go back over the lessons to check yourself.

1. Does Judy really like squash?

2. I just doubt that we can go with you tonight!

3. Why are bugs so attracted to bright lights?

4. The dog got stuck in the fence; he had to work and work before he got loose again.

5. I nearly fell over when I heard Bill won the prize.

6. Who did you say showed up unexpectedly at your house?

7. You will like that book from beginning to end!

8. Do you think I'm worried about you? Forget it!

9. Jack seems so worried about his job lately!

10. Judy and Jenny could hardly keep from laughing when Jack fell into the water!

11. Why does Bill want to get back at Bob?

12. Do you think you can resist the temptation?

13. This is a very hard job to do; it takes lots of patience!

14. It won't do you any good to butter up the boss; he's in a bad mood.

15. Did you blow your top at your friends for not showing up?

16. Please stop teasing Betty; she's easily embarrassed!

17. Jack and Jenny were fooling around the pond and Jenny pushed Jack in!

18. I.L.Y. buttons are on sale at the Bookstore.

19. Who gave you the authority to decide this?

20. I don't think you'll have much trouble finding the way.

21. Do you really want to go dancing?

22. O.K. We must stop this for now!

LESSON 16

MISCELLANEOUS IDIOMS

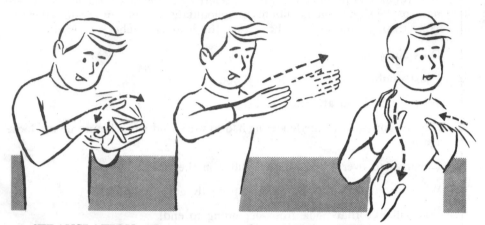

[TRANSLATION: "I am not sure about going to Chicago yet."]

1. Use the open-B" handshape, thumb at ear opening; move hand forward and back several times, holding thumb in original position, followed by "me". — I'm a "deafie". —or— I'm very very deaf!

2. Same position as above but move forward only once or start in forward position and move back up. — I haven't heard about that yet. —or— I know nothing about it.

3. Use the "1" handshape on the L hand and the "A" handshape on the R; with the R hand, knock on the "1"; add "you" or "me" or "him". — You are bluffing —or— You are fooling me! —or— You are trying to put something over on me.

4. Use the Dbl.-"C" under eyes with thumbs touching face below the eyes; move down to make eyes appear wide-open and haggard-looking. [Follow with "all night" and "me" to indicate being up all night.] — I was wide awake all night. —or— I couldn't sleep a wink! —or— I was up all night!

5. Use the thumb and index finger in a "G" position; place "G" at forehead, finger and thumb touching the head; move once to form a square at center of the forehead [often used in half-jest] — You are a square! —or— You are a numbskull! —or— You have no sense at all! —or— You have a bird brain!

6. Use Dbl. "L" handshape with the L's slightly crooked; place index fingers at ends of forehead; move straight out once rather vigorously; add "you". [This sign may also be made using the Dbl. "open-B" handshape.] — You are bigheaded! —or— You are very forward! —or— You think you're smart!

192

7. Use the "5" handshape on L hand, palm facing right and the crooked "2" handshape on R hand; move crooked "2" from thumb to index finger and on to other fingers. Indicate the subject. [This idiom is used to express the idea of moving from one thing to another, such as from one job to another or one person to another; not remaining stable.] — Joe jumps around from one job to another all the time. —or— My friends visited many different places in Washington.

8. Starting with the same position as above, move only to index finger and back to thumb; repeat movement a few times. Follow with "me" or other subject. — I move back and forth between these two jobs. —or— I do two jobs (indicate what) at the same time. —or— I alternate between these two jobs.

9. Use the "open-8" handshape in the taste position and bring it out with a fast shake or the hand; repeat 2 or 3 times; add "him" or "me". — He's very lucky! —or— I'm having a lot of fun with it!

10. Use the Dbl. "V" handshape, fingers pointing towards each other slightly with hands out near sides of the face; move fingers back past side of face quickly; add "me" and then "you" or yourself. — You flatter me! —or— I'm very flattered by what you said! —or— You flatter yourself!

11. Use the "5" handshape; place thumb on chest, fingers spread out; move hand up and out briskly, using appropriate expression of repulsiveness; add "me". — I resent that strongly! —or— I won't stand for that! —or— That (idea or thing) is positively repulsive to me!

12. Use the "2" handshape on the R hand and the "5" on the L hand, palm facing right; straddle the left index finger with the "2" and move back and forth. [This indicates being "on the fence" about something.] — I don't know yet —or— I haven't decided whether to or not. —or— I'm not sure.

13. Use the "Y" handshape at the right temple near the eye, 1 thumb touching face; move out sharply, either straight out or in sharp semi-circle. [This is often in talking about some food in response to "Do you like_____?] — I'm not crazy about that. —or— It's O.K., but I don't really care too much for it.

14. Use the "L" handshape, palm facing left; "shoot out" towards person you agree with as in seconding a motion, but with strong emphasis. [This sign looks almost like aiming a gun at someone] — I agree with you 100%! —or— I agree with you wholeheartedly. —or— I think exactly the same (as you do).

15. Use the Dbl. "open-B" handshape; one hand to each side of the face; move L hand down and R hand up simultaneously; then bend fingers and finish the "block" with R hand moving left and L hand moving right at top and bottom of face; add "you" or "me". — You are a blockhead!!!

16. Use the "C" handshape at lower lip, palm facing you; move out quickly to an "S" handshape. [This idiom is actually a sign for the idea of "cursing" someone or of feeling a vengeance against that person.] — I could curse you for talking too much! —or— I wish you'd keep your big mouth shut!

17. Use the "Y" handshape on the R hand and the "1" handshape on the L, palm facing you and finger pointing to the right; place the "Y" over L hand and move out along left index finger, wriggling R hand as you go. [This idiom is the sign for "cussing" or "swearing". A deaf person will often say: "Swear, swear, swear, me!" when making this idiom.] — I was so mad I just couldn't help swearing at him!

EXERCISES

Translate the following English sentences or ideas into sign language idioms or into approximate sign language colloquialisms. Names of persons may be spelled or you may point to another person in class as the subject of the sentence.

1. I'm not sure whether I should go or not.

2. You have no sense at all sometimes!

3. I agree with John 100%

4. I don't really care too much about asparagus. [Say "asparagus" first; then add the idiom.]

5. Joe thinks I'm a blockhead sometimes! He is bigheaded!

6. So you think you're so smart?

7. Are you trying to put something over on me?

8. Joe bluffs his friends about his wrestling victories!

9. Joe says he resents that strongly!

10. Josephine keeps going around with different men all the time!

11. Some people like to move around from one job to another.

12. Do you like to visit around different places?

13. Geraldine was flattered when Bob proposed!

14. Don't try flattering me!

15. Joe is having a lot of fun with his little tricks!

16. Jerry's very lucky, really!

17. Jenny couldn't sleep a wink all night long!

18. You stayed up all night? That was stupid!

19. Bob can really be very deaf when he wants to!

20. No, we've heard absolutely nothing about it!

21. Joe sometimes does two different jobs at the same time.

22. I couldn't help swearing at the dog; I was so mad at him for tearing up my flowers!

LESSON 17

MISCELLANEOUS IDIOMS

1. "_____, carry hospital." Here use the Dbl. "2" handshape, fingers pointing out; bring up quickly to crooked "2"s; followed by signs for "carry to hospital"; indicate subject. — He was hurt badly and taken to the hospital —or— He was suddenly stricken and rushed to the hospital.

2. "_____, me!" Use the same sign and movement as above, followed by "me". — I am dead tired now! —or— I am completely exhausted!

3. "_____, sick!" or "Sick_____!" Use the same sign and movement, followed by "him". — He became seriously ill all of a sudden!

4. "_____, him!" Use the same sign and movement here as in No. 1, but you move "2"s up more slowly and then hold crooked "2"s stiffly for a moment; add subject. [NOTE: the sign <u>die</u> is also used in this way; the above gesture is more of a slang sign for <u>die</u>.] — He died suddenly! —or— He just dropped dead!

5. Use the Dbl. "5" handshape, fingers crooked and palms facing each other; twist both hands simultaneously but in opposite directions. [Indicate what is "fouled up", "ruined", or "wrecked".] — Everything is all fouled up! —or— The whole thing is one big mess!

6. Use the Dbl. "A" handshape, holding L hand above R hand, palms facing each other; bring together sharply, lifting R hand to strike against the L; add "you", "me", etc. — You are a nitwit! —or— What a dumbell you are! —or— You are so stupid!

7. Use the "5" handshape on R hand; bring fingers down over face as in signing "sleep"; change immediately to Dbl. "A" handshape as in #6, R hand down to L; add "me" or "you", plus "when!". — I fell soundly asleep! —or— I slept like a log! —or— I was dead to the world!

8. Use the Dbl. "S" handshape, palms facing each other; open to a Dbl. "5" handshape as you bring hands sharply and quickly together; add "the two of us", "we", or "they". — We had a bad fight! —or— We clashed over the incident. (issue, or whatever it may have been)

9. Use the Dbl. "5" handshape with the L hand facing palm down and the R hand placed under the L, palm facing you; hold L hand steady and move R hand in small circles indicating a "flame" burning under L hand; add "me". —I was boiling mad about that! —or— That just burns me up!

10. Use the "open-8" handshape, middle finger touching left temple; sweep across the forehead to the right; add "me" or "you", etc. — I completely forgot all about this! —or— My mind draws a complete blank. —or— I can't remember one thing about it.

11. Use "F" handshape sidewise in front of chin; bring the "F" quickly to the chin; add "me", etc. — I'm an expert at this! —or— This is no problem for me to handle.

12. Use same sign as above, adding the sign for words like "talk", "lie", or "cover up", [See description in #14], etc; add "you" or "me", etc. — You are a big talker! —or— You are an expert liar! —or— You really know how to talk!

13. Use the Dbl. "1" handshape, fingers pointing back at sides of head; move quickly back past head simultaneously; add "me". — I don't understand one thing (he is saying). —or— I was paying attention but was not listening.

14. Use the Dbl. "5" handshape, palms facing each other, but with R hand thumb touching little finger of the L hand; brush hands past each other; add, for example "talk" plus "you" or "him", etc. — You are trying to cover up something. —or— You are hiding something from me (us). —or— You are not telling the whole truth.

15. Use "A" handshape, thumb up; move hand forward shortly and briskly with a smile. [This sign may have come from the old Irish greeting: "Top o' the morning (day, evening) to you!"] — So long until later! —or— So long! See you later! —or— Good luck! See you around!

16. Use the "5" handshape on L hand, palm facing upward, and the "Open-8" handshape on the R hand; place right middle finger in center of L palm and sweep back towards yourself. Add "me". [This idiom refers to the idea of "taking advantage of someone or something.] — I'm taking advantage of this!

EXERCISES

Translate the following English sentences or ideas into sign language idioms or into approximate sign language colloquialisms. Names of persons may be spelled or you may point to another person in class as the subject of the sentence.

1. Jimmy is all in from that hard job!

2. John had a heart attack and was rushed to the hospital last night!

3. Were you really very sick?

4. He simply dropped dead just like that!

5. So long, friend! See you around!

6. It looks like the whole situation is one big beautiful mess!

7. Sometimes kids seem so stupid!

8. The minute I hit the pillow, I was dead to the world!

9. Joe and his wife had a bad spat the other day.

10. That talk just burns me up!

11. I'm sorry but the appointment simply slipped my mind; I was so busy!

12. Jack thinks he can handle the problem easily!

13. You are one big talker; half of what you say is not true!

14. All through the lecture, Bill sat daydreaming; he got nothing out of class!

15. I think Jim is covering up for somebody!

16. Bill and Bob like to take advantage of the girls; they think it's fun!

17. You should take advantage of your opportunities while you're young!

18. What are you trying to hide from me now?

19. It looks like McGovern and Nixon are going to clash before election day!

20. I was thinking about nothing in particular, really!

LESSON 18

MISCELLANEOUS IDIOMS

1. Dbl. "B" handshape, palms facing downward; place hands against sides of stomach; move up slowly at first and finish with a vigorous upward sweep into the air. [The movement illustrates slowly rising anger or frustration that suddenly explodes.] — I was so mad I simply blew up! —or— That made me boiling mad!

2. Use the "1" handshape; position in front of face, palm facing left; move back to lips in one hard movement and add "me". — I didn't mean that! —or— Why did I do this that way? (I didn't mean to.)

3. Use the Dbl. "1" handshape pointing a finger in each ear as in "hear"; move directly out from the ear opening into a Dbl. "5" handshape palms facing upward. — I don't care! —or— I dare to! —or— I'm not afraid to do (try) that!

4. Spell "Do-do-do?" (rapidly), palms facing upwards. [NOTE: This idiom is used when one suddenly finds himself in an awkward or embarrassing position that he wants to get out of right away.] — What shall I (we) do?

   [Alter the idiom; try spelling "do-do-do, night, you?"] — What are you doing tonight? —or— Do you have any plans for tonight?

5. Use the "shot H" sign for "beat you". This is made by holding index and fingers under thumb, R palm facing left, and "shooting out" to an "H". Add "me" or reverse it and say "Beat me, you!", followed by "whew!" — I'm better than you are! —or— I'm better than you at this game! —or— You are better than me! —or— You will beat me at this game easily!

6. Precede the "shot H" with sign: "mine". [This is not to be interpreted literally.] — Mine is better than yours! —or— My (car) (TV) (Daddy) is better than yours!

7. Follow the "shot H" with the idiomatic sign for "expert". [SEE No. 11 in Lesson 17] — I can beat you any old time! —or— I can outdo you easily.

8. Use the Dbl. "F" handshape, palms facing each other; shake hands back and forth sidewise 2 or 3 times; add "you", "him", etc. — You are nothing to be afraid of! —or— You are no challenge! —or— You are a nobody!

9. Use the Dbl. "C" handshape; alternately sign "hungry" with first the R hand and then the L; add "you", "him", or "me". [Most often used in jest or teasing.] — Boy! Are you passionate! —or— You are full of desire! —or— He is filled with passion (desire)!

10. Use the "5" handshape, thumb on chest as in "fine"; instead of moving out, wiggle the fingers, holding thumb in position; add "you" or "him", etc. [This expression is frequently used as a reaction to some humorous human error or joke or to a clever or witty remark made by someone.] — [No real English equivalent can be expressed here; however, the following examples might do.] You are really cool! —or— You are really something!

11. Sign as above but with more emphasis; then add or indicate to whom or what you are referring. — (Joe) is a swell guy! I really like him! —or— This is the best (saw) I ever had!

12. Use the "crooked-5" handshape on the R hand and the "1" on the L hand; place the "1" in front of you; move the "5" so that it almost surrounds the "1". Add "you", "me", "him", etc., followed by "whew!" [NOTE: Another way to say this is to use the same basic movement as for "famous", but move out only once instead of twice.] — You are really popular! —or— Wow! What a lot of admirers you have!

13. Use the base sign for "taste" on the chin; follow by signing "my" + "not", add "you" or "him". — You are not my type —or— He (she) is not exactly my kind of company.

14. Use the Dbl. "5" handshape, palms facing downward and fingers pointing out; move forward wiggling fingers up and down; indicate place or occasion and add "whew!" — Boy! What a crowd there was at that movie! —or— An overflow crowd was at the game (show)!

15. Use the "5" handshape on the L hand, palm facing right, and the "crooked-2" on the R; place the "2" at the left little finger; move up past all fingers; add "wish" (with emphasis) + "me". — I really wish I could go to the top! —or— I really desire to move up (in my position or job).

16. The same idea may be conveyed by using the basic sign for "thirst" in place of "wish"; also with emphasis, and followed by the idiom "moving up". [Other ideas may be substituted for "going to the top" or "moving up in rank", such as "travel", for example.] — I really wish I could be free to travel around! —or— There is nothing I'd like better than to be able to travel.

17. Use the Dbl. "Y" handshape, hands out and palms facing downward; move hands in small circles towards and away from each other several times. [Denotes the same old "record" being played over and over.] — It's the same old thing over and over!

EXERCISES

Translate the following English sentences or ideas into sign language idioms or into approximate sign language colloquialisms. Names of persons may be spelled or you may point to another person in class as the subject of the sentence.

1. Oh, what shall we do now? The boss is coming!
   - [Pretend you're playing a game of cards on the job and don't have time to get them out of the way so the boss won't know it!)

2. I wasn't afraid to try that!

3. My daddy is better than your daddy!

4. Joe is better than you at this game, I think!

5. That is the best car I've ever seen!

6. Jim thinks Bob is a great player. Do you agree?

7. Last night was really one swell evening, wasn't it?

8. Boy, that was a clever remark you made!

9. Jim was so mad at Bill last night, he literally blew up!

10. I'm sorry, I didn't mean to say that at all!

11. What do you think we should do tonight?

12. Bob thinks he can easily beat Joe any old time!

13. In other words, Bob thinks Joe is nothing!

14. You really seem to be filled with desire. Cool it!

15. Joe doesn't think Betty is really Bob's type!

16. Did you see that crowd on U.S. 1 last night?

17. Bob hopes to move up in his job before long.

18. Most of us really wish we were free to travel the world!

19. I like to work at many different jobs all the time.

20. I don't like doing the same old thing all the time; it gets boring!

PRACTICE TEST 6

Lessons 16 - 17 - 18

Go through this practice test without referring back to the last three lessons to see how many of the sign language idioms or colloquialisms you can recall. After you have gone through the test, go back over the lessons to check yourself.

1. You mean to say you've heard nothing about the fire?

2. Don't you get tired of the same old problems over and over?

3. I don't know why but everything seems to be a complete mess!

4. What are you trying to put over on me now?

5. It's hard to get around to see all the famous places in Washington in a short time.

6. Bob wouldn't go along with our plans; he said he resented the idea!

7. Why did Jim suddenly become very sick at the party?

8. What made you two clash over that small thing?

9. Think you can beat me at this game?

10. Jim completely forgot about his date with Judy!

11. Do you two have any plans for Friday night?

12. I don't consider a Volkswagen my type of car!

13. Remember the times when women just flocked to see Elvis Presley?

14. If you want to get ahead in your job, you have to work!

15. Don't you want to take advantage of this opportunity?

16. Bill and Bob haven't decided yet whether or not to go fishing Saturday.

17. I wish you hadn't done that!

18. What are you trying to cover up now?

19. Bob used to be an expert at hitting a strike. (bowling)

20. The other day I dropped off to sleep like a log; I was that tired!

21. Can you tell me what made you so boiling mad?

22. I'm sorry, I didn't mean it that way!

BIBLIOGRAPHY

The works listed in this bibliography represent recent publications as well as materials out of print. Some of the publications are suitable for teaching, others for research, and a third group cater mainly to specialized interests such as those on underwater signs and those on hymn signing. Specific information is available from the National Association for the Deaf or from the Gallaudet College Sign Language Programs.

1. Babbini, Barbara E. *An Introductory Course in Manual Communication: Fingerspelling and the Language of Signs.* Northridge, California: California State University at Northridge, 1965. (San Fernando Valley State College)

    Babbini, Barbara E. *Manual Communication: Fingerspelling and the Language of Signs: A Course of Study Outline for Students.* Champagne, Illinois: University of Illinois Press, 1972-1973.

    Babbini, Barbara E. *Manual Communication: Fingerspelling and the Language of Signs: A Course of Study Outline for Instructors.* Champagne, Illinois: University of Illinois Press, 1972-1973.

2. Baynes, H.L. *Basic Signs.* (Publication Information is unavailable. One pamphlet in Gallaudet College Library.) Out of Print.

3. Becker, Valentine A. *Underwater Sign Language.* (Catalog No. 1919, U.S. Divers Corps. Write to the author, Supervisor of Physically Handicapped, Public School System, San Francisco, California.)

4. Benson, Elizabeth. *Sign Language.* St. Paul, Minnesota: St. Paul Technical Vocational Institute.

5. Bornstein, Harry, Lillian B. Hamilton, and Barbara M. Kannapell. *Signs for Instructional Purposes.* Washington, D.C.: Gallaudet College Press, 1969.

6. Casterline, Dorothy, Carl C. Croneberg, and William C. Stokoe, Jr. *A Dictionary of American Sign Language on Linguistic Principles.* Washington, D.C.: Gallaudet College Press, 1965.

7. Cissna, Roy. *Basic Sign Language.* Jefferson City, Missouri: Missouri Baptist Convention, 1963. Out of Print.

8. Davis, Anne. *The Language of Signs.* New York, New York: Executive Council of the Episcopal Church, 1966.

9. Delaney, Theo and C. Bailey. *Sing Unto the Lord: A Hymnal for the Deaf.* (Hymns translated into signs.) Ephphetha Conference of Lutheran Pastors for the Deaf, 1959.

10. Falberg, Roger M. *The Language of Silence.* Wichita, Kansas: Wichita Social Services for the Deaf, 1963.

11. Fant, Louis J. *Say It With Hands*. Washington, D.C.: American Annals of the Deaf, Gallaudet College, 1964.

12. Fauth, Bette La Verne and Warren Wesley Fauth. "A Study of Proceedings of the Convention of American Instructors of the Deaf, 1850-1949, IV," Chapter XIII, "The Manual Alphabet," *American Annals of the Deaf*, 96:292-296, March 1951. (Bibliography included.)

13. Fauth, Bette La Verne and Warren Wesley Fauth. "Sign Language," *American Annals of the Deaf*, 100:253-263, March 1955.

14. Geylman, I. "The Sign Language and Hand Alphabet of Deaf Mutes," *Proceedings of the Workshop on Interpreting for the Deaf*. Muncie, Indiana: Ball State Teachers College, 1964. pp. 62-90.

15. Guillory, La Vera M. *Expressive and Receptive Fingerspelling for Hearing Adults*. Baton Rouge, Louisiana: Claitor's Book Store, 1966.

16. Higgins, Daniel, C.S.S.R. *How to Talk to the Deaf*. Newark, New Jersey: Mount Carmel Guild, Archdiocese of Newark, 1959.

17. Hoemann, Harry W., Ed. *Improved Techniques of Communication: A Training Manual for Use with Severly Handicapped Deaf Clients*. Bowling Green, Ohio: Bowling Green State University, 1970.

18. Jordan, Florence. *Lesson Outlines for Teaching and the Study of Dactylology*.

19. Kosche, Martin. *Hymns for Singing and Signing*. Delavan, Wisconsin.

20. Landes, Robert M. *Approaches: A Digest of Methods in Learning the Language of Signs*. Richmond, Virginia: 1968.

21. Long, J. Schuyler. *The Sign Language: A Manual of Signs*. Washington, D.C.: Gallaudet College, 1962. (Reprint of second edition.) Out of Print.

22. Michaels, J.W. *A Handbook of the Sign Language*. Atlanta: Home Mission Board, Southern Baptist Convention, 1923. Out of Print.

23. O'Rourke, Terrence J., Ed. *A Basic Course in Manual Communication*. National Association of the Deaf, Communicative Skills Program, Silver Spring, Maryland, 1970.

24. Peet, Elizabeth. "The Philology of the Sign Language," *Buff and Blue*. Gallaudet College, March 1921. (Reprinted in pamphlet form by Gallaudet College.) Out of Print.

25. Rand, Lawrence W. *An Annotated Bibliography of the Sign Language of the Deaf*. Seattle, Washington: University of Washington, 1962. (Unpublished M.A. Thesis.)

26. Riekehof, Lottie L. *Talk to the Deaf.* Springfield, Missouri: Gospel Publishing House, 1963.

27. Roth, Stanley D. *A Basic Book of Signs Used by the Deaf.* Fulton, Missouri: Missouri School for the Deaf, 1948. Out of Print.

28. Sanders, Josef I., Ed. *The ABC's of Sign Language.* Tulsa, Oklahoma: Manca Press, 1968.

29. Siger, Leonard C. "Gestures, the Language of Signs, and Human Communication," *American Annals of the Deaf,* 113:11-28, January 1968.

30. Springer, C.S., C.S.S.R. *Talking With the Deaf.* Baton Rouge, Louisiana: Redemptorist Fathers, 1961.

31. Stokoe, W.C. *Sign Language Structure: An Outline of the Visual Communication Systems of the American Deaf.* Buffalo, New York: University of Buffalo, 1960.

32. Watson, David. *Talk With Your Hands.* Menasha, Wisconsin: George Banta Publishing Co., 1963.

33. Wisher, Peter R. *Use of the Sign Language in Underwater Communication.* Washington, D.C.: Lithography by Gallaudet College.

The following indexes to the *American Annals of the Deaf* indicate additional references to articles in the *Annals* that deal with sign language. The page numbers given refer to the pages in the indexes on which these articles are listed.

Index No.	Page No.
I	40-45
II	85-87
III	86
IV	75
V	78
VI	433
VII	537-538
VIII	545
IX	404

Index Number 10 has not yet been published. The Volume numbers and pagination for articles on manual communication which have appeared in the *Annals* since 1956 are listed below.

Volume No.	Page no.
101	245-254
103	264-282
	524-525
104	232-240
105	232-237
	434
106	11-28
109	364-366
110	483-485
	585
111	452-460
	499-504
	557-565
113	11-28
	29-41
	975-977
115	497-498
	527-536
116	434-436
117	20-24
	27-33

INDEX TO SIGNS

ninety-seven, 20
ninety-eight, 20
noon, 10
Norway, 40
a notice, 86
notice (verb), 86
notify, 73
now and then, 126
number (s) and figures, 22
nurse, 49

objective, 76
obey, 73
observe, 58
occasionally, 12
of (possessive), 94
off and on, 81, 133
often, 11
Old Maid, 49
Oldsmobile (car), 25
on the whole, 131
once, 12
once and for all, 133
once in a while, 12, 126
one, 18
one-fourth (1/4), 21
one hundred (100), 19
one hundred percent (100%), 21
one thousand, 19
one week ago, 11
onions, 29
operation, 51
opportunity, 70
oranges, 33
order, 91
our own, 66
out-of-order, 128
over and over, 12, 128
overcome, 91
overflow, 84
overlook, 84
own, 66
oysters, 29

park — your car, 25,
park — here, 25
park near the street, 25
parking, 25
parking lot, 25
parking ticket, 25

parlor, 36
pastor, 48
patio, 36
patronize, 133
pay attention, 61, 126
pay attention to me, 61
peaches, 32
peas, 29
a penny, 16
pepper, 32
Percent (s), 22
perfect, 67
perilous, 95
permit, 70, 89
personality, 69
persuade/persuasion, 78
Philadelphia, 42
pianist, 48
pick out, 124
pick up, 116
pie, 31
pilot, 48
Pittsburgh, 42
plate, 37
player, 48
plenty, 83
pneumonia, 51
poet, 48
point out, 124
policeman, 49
political affiliation, 53
politician, 53
politics, 53
pop up, 18
position, 69
Positive vs. Negative, 66
possessives, 66
possible/possibility, 78
post-, 64
potatoes, 29
pounds, 69
powder room, 36
prairie, 94
pre-, 64
Prefixes, 64
preacher, 48
precise, 67
prefer, 89
Presbyterian, 44
president, 53

213

214

situation, 70
six, 18
sixteen, 18
sixty-six, 19
sixty-seven, 20
sixty-eight, 20
sixty-nine, 20
skid (in a car), 26
slow traffic, 26
smart/smarter/smartest, 56
so-so, 81, 133
so far, 126
soft boiled eggs, 31
sometimes, 12
soup, 31
sour cream, 30
Southeastern University, 44
spacious, 94
Spain, 40
spangled, 96
speaker, 48
spinach, 30
spinster, 49
spoon, 37
stand for, 135
stand out, 124
stand up, 118
star, 96
"The Star Spangled Banner", 95
St. Louis, 42
stay up, 118
statement, 78
stick/stick to, 131
stick up, 116
stir up, 116
stranger, 49
strawberries, 34
streaming (in shooting), 96
strict, 86
strike (go on strike), 81
strike out, 124
string beans, 29
stripes, 97
student, 49
Suffixes, 64
sufficient, 83
sugar, 32
sun, 73
supervisor, 49
support, 70

suppose (verb), 57
suppose to, 57
surgeon, 48
surgery, 51
suspect/suspicion, 75
Sweden, 40
swimmer, 48
syrup, 32

take — a course, 101
take after — one's father, 101
take after — in skill, 101
take down — notes, 101
take down drapes, 101
take down a number, 101
take off (as in an airplane), 101
take off — clothes, 101
take on (behavior), 101
take on (in hiring), 101
take out — a book, 101
take out — a friend, 101
take me (us) out, 101
take out a part, 101
take out the trash, 101
take up — golf, 101
take up — a matter, 101
take a look at, 103
take a part in, 103
take apart, 103
take hold of, 103
take it easy, 103
take my place, 103
take over a country, 103
take over — for someone, 103
take pity on, 103
take sides, 103
take time off, 103
take a seat, 102
take a walk, 102
take turns, 102
tea, 30
tear down, 105
tear up, 105
telephone numbers, 23
temple, 45
ten, 18
tend to/tendency, 78
than, 73
the day after tomorrow, 11
the day before yesterday, 10

INDEX TO PART III

[NOTE: Idioms for which there are no "broken English" expressions are **not** included here.]

Page #141

"Bother, go away.", "Bother, finish."
"Eat, finish, you?", "You finish eat?"
"Finish see you?", "See finish, you?"
"Heard finish before me."
"Heard finish before, you?"
"Laugh at me, finish!"
"Me finish!"
"Play, play, finish!"
"See finish, me.", "See finish yesterday."

Page #142

"Apply finish, me."
"_____ all gone, finish!"
"(He, it, etc.) gone finish!"; (zoom) (whew!)
"Me finish!!!"
"School finish, zoom, me!"
"Time finish!"
"Train gone (zoom) finish, sorry!"
"You-me race; me gone (zoom) finish!"

Page #144

"Inform you, finish me!"
"Mail letter yesterday, finish me!"
"My car worn out finish!"
"Once, finish. Again not have to!"
"Pay off (loan) yesterday, finish me."
"Plan, plan, wrecked finish!"
"Ready finish, wish me!"
"Ready test finish, wish you?"
"Tease me, finish you!"

Page #145

"Altogether how many (problems) finish, you?"
"Bawl out (him/her) finish you?"
"Finish, finish, please!"
"Go, go, many times, finish, me!"
"I,I,I, finish, you!"
"Money earn finish, how much you?"
"Puzzled, finish me. Whew!"

Page #147

"Bawl out him, late, you!"
"Decide late, me."
"Eager! Late, you!"
"Give me, late, you!"
"Hear late me."
"Inform me, late you!"
"Late eat, me (you)."
"Late write, me late.", "Late write me.
  No time!"
"Learn (_____) late, me?"
"Man pop up, late."
"See late, me."
"Think late, me."
"Time finish, late!"

Page #148

"Late teach me, late, you!"
"Laugh at (him) late, me!"

Page #151

"Mind frozen, me!"
"Mind limit, me (you)!"
"Mind stunned, me!"
"Think easy, you?"
"Think funny, you"
"Think (mind)_____, you?"
"Think snow night, you think?"
"Think, think___?___you?"
"Think, you?"
"Think zero, me!"

Page #152

"Important, think you?"
"Learn, learn, can't me; mind limit!"
"Think (mind) strong, me."
"Think nothing, you?"
"Think yourself!"

Page #154

"Ambition zero, me!"
"Eager zero, me!"
"Feel comfortable, zero, me!"
"Funny zero."
"Give me zero!"
"Have zero, me!"
"Interest zero, me!"
"John funny zero football!"

"Like zero!"
"Money zero, me!"
"Patience zero, me!"
"Pity zero, me!"
"Respect zero, me!"
"Understand zero, me!"

Page #155

"Excuse zero, you!"
"Feel zero, me!"
"Wrong zero!"

Page #157

"Feel_____, me!"
"Feel deflated me."
"Feel good, me!"
"Feel lousy, me!"
"Feel tough, me!"
"Heart, him, whew!"
"Heart me, whew!"
"Heart soft, you!"
"Heart zero, you!"
"Pity you, me!"

Page #158

"Feel about $3—$4."
"Feel come them, feel me."
"Feel pass, you?"
"Feel strong win, me!"

Page #161

"Imagination, succeed you!"
"Laugh, succeed you!"
"Pop up, succeed you!"
"Red face, succeed you, me!"
"Succeed fail, me."
"Succeed, finish, late me!"
"Succeed, finish me!"
"Succeed hit me!"
"Succeed late, you!"
"Succeed letter get, me, succeed!"
"Succeed on time, you!"
"Succeed strike, me!"
"Succeed, time!"
"Study, study, succeed you!"
"Support me, succeed you!"
"Work, succeed you!"

Page #163

"Lie down minute, why not you?"
"Lying (flat on back), me!"

Page #164

"Lie down, can't me!"
"Lie down quiet, me, dreaming."

Page #166

"Blame, blame, me, why (for-for)?"
"Eager, you, for-for?"
"Face expression, for-for (why)?"
"For-for?"
"Hungry, hungry, for-for?"
"Laugh at me, for-for?"
"Red faced, for-for?"
"Talk, talk, for-for?"
"Work, work, for-for?"

Page #167

"Foolish, foolish, for-for?"
"Funny! For-for (why)?"
"Go, for-for?"
"Imagination you, for-for (why)?"
"Money, money, for-for?"
"Stay up all night, for-for?"
"Worry, worry, for-for?"

Page #170

"Disgusted, me!"
"Fault (blame) yourself!"
"Hypocrite, you!"
"I,I,I, you!"
"Me sick that!"
"Me sick, you!"
"Selfish, you!"
"Stomach turnover, me!"
"Stink you!"
"Vomit, me!"

Page #171

"Embarrassed, me!"
"Famous late you, famous!"
"Imagination, stop (finish)!"
"Imagination, too much, you!"
"Look up and down at you, me!"
"Nervy (bold) (fresh), you!"

"Red face, you!"
"Strict, you! Whew!"
"Stupid, you!"
"Tough, him (you, me, etc.)"

Page #174

I. The "Worthless/Useless" Pattern:

II. The "Why Not" Pattern:

"Play, why not, you?"
"Support me, why not, you?"
"Why not teach me, why not you?"

III. The "Won't Me" Pattern:

"Forgive, won't me!"
"Help, won't me!"

Page #175

IV. The "Will You" Pattern:

"Lose, will you!"
"Mad, will you?"
"Sick, will you!"
"Sorry, will you!"

Page #177

I. The "Hungry/Wish" Pattern:

"Go, wish, you?"
"Hungry, me!"
"Hungry, you?"

II. The "Whew" Pattern:

"Awful, whew!"
"Beautiful, whew!"
"Funny you, whew!"

Page #178 — The "Whew" Pattern continued

"Eager, me, whew!"
"Interest me, whew!"
"Look strong father, you! Whew!
   Wrong, zero!"

III. The "Money" Pattern:

"Altogether, how much worth (money), figure you?"
"Money comfortable, you!"
"Money earn many, guess, you!"
"Money, many?"
"Money much (or lots), they."

IV. The "Questioning" Pattern:

"Funny!"
"Strange (odd), true!"

Page #181

I. The "You???" Pattern:

"Busy, you??"
"Eager, you??"
"Laugh you?? Phooey!"
"Like, you??"
"Think you?? Phooey!"
"Worry, you?? Phooey!"

II. More Simple "ME" Patterns:

"Angry, me!"
"Not like, me!"
"Sorry, me!" (2)
"Worry, me? Phooey!"
"Worry, me, whew!"

Page #182 More Simple "ME" Patterns

"Resist, me!"
"Tired out, me!"

III. A "Mimic" Idiom Pattern:

"Cut it!"

Page #184

I. More Simple "ME" Patterns:

"Disbelieve, me!" (2)
"Heard never before, me!"
"Support me, you?"

II. Varied Compound Patterns:

"Get even him, hungry (wish) me!"
"Look at me, stop, not nice!"
"Pop up, not expect!"

III. Repeating Patterns:

"Foolish, foolish, foolish, me!"
"Me bawl out, bawl out him!"

Page #185 More Repeating Patterns:

"Blame, blame me, always, they!"
"Earn, earn, earn, me!"
"Hard, hard, hard, hard; not easy!"
"Struggle, struggle fix, fail, me!"
"Struggle, struggle -- succeed fix, finish me!"
"Work, work, work, me!"

220